D1045614

·GREEK·
LEGENDS

TOP·TEN

·GREEK·
LEGENDS

TERRY DEARY

Illustrated by **Michael Tickner**

Hippo

For the legendary Sian Allen

Scholastic Children's Books,
Commonwealth House, 1-19 New Oxford Street, London WC1A 1NU, UK

A division of Scholastic Ltd
London ~ New York ~ Toronto ~ Sydney ~ Auckland

Published in the UK by Scholastic Ltd, 1998

Text copyright © Terry Deary, 1998
Illustrations copyright © Michael Tickner, 1998

All rights reserved

ISBN 0 590 193775

Typeset by Rapid Reprographics Ltd
Printed and bound by Nørhaven Paperback A/S, Denmark

13 15 17 19 20 18 16 14

The right of Terry Deary and Michael Tickner to be identified as the author and illustrator of
this work respectively has been asserted by them in accordance with the Copyright, Designs and
Patents Act, 1988.

This book is sold subject to the condition that it shall not, by way of trade or otherwise be lent,
resold, hired out, or otherwise circulated without the publisher's prior consent in any form of
binding other than that in which it is published and without a similar condition, including this
condition, being imposed upon the subsequent purchaser.

Contents

Introduction

It's amazing ... but true. Some people are so *old* they lived in the days before everyone had a television! You may even *know* some of these people – a grandparent, a teacher – or a mummy in your local museum. Next time you meet them ask, "What did you do before you had a television?"

You'll find they usually say, "We sat around the fire and talked". (Don't make any remarks about them painting the walls of their caves ... they probably aren't *that* old.)

They may even say, "We told stories".

People have told stories since ancient times. They told them to try to explain the world around them. That flaming ball in the sky above them, the mysterious flashes and crashing sounds of a storm; the blood-drinking, flesh-tearing terrors that lived in the forests and the magical mysteries of fire and floods and fifty thousand other fears that haunted their dreams.

Above all they wondered about birth and death. Is this the only world and the only life? Or is there something

7

more? Is there another better world to look forward to ... or a worse one where the terrors of your nightmares really do come true.

When darkness fell and these people stopped work for the day, they sat around their fire and they talked, and they listened. Someone would be a better talker than the others and someone would begin telling stories.

These stories would be remembered and passed on. Or they would be heard by travellers and carried to nearby lands and repeated and changed.

In time humans learned to write and someone wrote the stories down so that people of the future could read them.

You are the people of that future. They never guessed that you would be able to read their stories three thousand years after they wrote them ... but I'll bet they'd be thrilled at the thought!

There are too many stories to fit into one book, so here are just 10 from the ancient Greeks: the Top 10. They are retold in a new form as modern stories and there are also additional top 10 sections of Top Facts for you to dip into and learn more about the Greeks and their pleasures and their problems.

So here are the Top 10 Greek legends – in reverse order, of course!

Legend 10: Zeus

Greek myths are fun because the gods are fun. They are the most dishonest, cruel and lawless bunch of characters you could ever want to meet. And they had so much power!

The most powerful Greek god was the most ruthless of all. His name was Zeus and he was top dog – or should that be top *god* – and his story is number 10 in our chart of top legends. Zeus was also a big spoilt kid. Whatever he wanted, he got. If he didn't get it then he sulked . . . or cheated . . . or turned very nasty until he *did* get it.

Imagine being married to a character like that! Hera was. She *must* have had a tough life, trying to live with a god like that . . .

Hera's tale

My mother warned me, "Marry that Zeus and he'll bring you nothing but trouble. You mark my words." A girl should always listen to her mother.

Some of you may have heard the story about my dad, Cronos, and how he chewed up all of his children as soon as they were born? You haven't? Oh, well, Cronos's trouble-making mother told him that one of his children would grow up to throw him off his throne. So, every time a child was born, he ate it! Our mum, Rhea, got fed up with this and fed Cronos a rock dressed in baby clothes. The old cannibal ate the rock and the baby lived.

That baby was Zeus, of course. Zeus took ten years to throw the old gods out but he did it in the end. Then he looked around for a wife. As human beings hadn't been invented he had to marry a goddess and he picked me for my beauty, my brains and because there wasn't a lot of choice.

Now I was Zeus's sister, you understand. I guess you girls would not fancy marrying a brother – well, I suppose your brothers wouldn't think much of marrying you! The trouble started when I married Zeus.

He married me which means we stay together till death do us part. And, since we gods live forever, that's an awfully long time. But Zeus gets bored easily. He's not satisfied with a beautiful, intelligent wife like me. Oh, no. He has to go flirting with any female that takes his fancy. The trouble I've had with him and his girlfriends.

Take Princess Io of the Peloponnese. A lovely human girl – hair black as a raven's wing and skin as soft as a pig's tail.

"I'm just off to the Peloponnese, my sweet little porcupine," Zeus said one morning.

"Why?" I asked.

His mouth fell open, then his bottom lip wobbled the way it always does when he's going to tell a lie. "Fishing," he said.

"Where's your net?" I asked.

"Er . . . not using a net, pet," he chuckled. "Thought I'd just send down a few thunderbolts."

"That's cheating a bit, isn't it?" I asked him.

He blew out his fat red cheeks. "Ooooh! Not really. Some of those little beggars dart about a lot. It's good target practice for me."

I nodded. "Bring me back a haddock," I said as he rose up into the clouds above Olympus.

He waved and drifted off singing, "I-o, I-o, it's off to fish we go!"

"I-o?" I thought. "I've heard that name somewhere. Then I remembered Princess Io. One of the daimons told me about her. Every human has two daimons – a good spirit and a bad spirit – and they gossip terribly. This Io was beautiful, they said. Even a one-eyed Cyclops could see what Zeus was up to.

"I'll fettle him and stop his little games," I muttered and took the fastest horse I could find. As we reached the Peloponnese plain I stopped on top of a mountain overlooking the seashore and there he was, disguised as a human, and talking to a woman.

The horse gave a small whinny, Zeus turned round and saw me as I galloped down the ridge. I jumped off the horse and glared at him as he stood there with his arm around the neck of a cow.

"What are you up to?" I demanded.

The cow said, "Moo!"

Zeus smiled, "Just admiring this beautiful cow, my sweet little cobra!"

The cow said, "Moo!"

I could see what had happened. He'd used his divine power to turn the princess into a cow. As soon as I left he'd change her back into a woman. I wasn't having that. I said, "I-o."

Zeus said, "What!"

The cow said, "Moo!"

"I-o. I-o . . . I-o-nly hope you've got my haddock," I said sweetly.

"Haddock?"

"You were going fishing," I reminded him.

"Left Olympus without me thunderbolts," he sighed. "Sorry, my little pot of petunias."

I smiled a wide and beautiful smile. "So you decided to give me this wonderful cow instead!" I cried.

"Did I?" my hateful husband muttered.

"Of course you did!" I sighed. "I am so lucky to have such a thoughtful husband."

"You can't take the cow back to Olympus. Not a lot of grass on our mountain top," he said quickly.

"You're right. I'll leave it here but have a very special friend of mine to look after it."

"You have a friend?" Zeus said through clenched teeth.

"Argus. He'll keep an eye on it!" I said and laughed.

"Very funny," my simmering spouse said. As you know, Argus would keep more than *an eye* on the cow. Because Argus has dozens of eyes! All over his body in fact. This caused him a lot of teasing when he went to school, of course. Lots of jokes about throwing him out of the class because there were too many pupils for the teacher to cope with. Eyes – pupils, get it? Oh, never mind.

So I called on dear Argus and gave him the job. "But watch out for Zeus. He'll try any mean trick in the book to steal that cow away from under your very eyes," I warned him.

"Don't worry, missis," Argus sniffed. "All my eyes never go to sleep at the same time."

"Good lad," I winked. Argus tried to wink back but he looked a blinking fool.

I went back to Olympus happily and Zeus sulked. I gave him steak pie for tea and said the meat came from a freshly sacrificed cow. I let him choke on a mouthful of meat before I said, "But not from the dear little cow you gave me, of course."

He glared at me and left the table without even drinking his nectar. I think he was off his food. What a baby.

As I expected it didn't take Zeus long to try and steal Io back. He couldn't get away to the Peloponnese coast himself so he sent our son Hermes to do his dirty work. I have to admit I was careless then. I was sure Hermes would never send Argus to sleep but I was wrong.

Our boy disguised himself as a shepherd and took some magic pipes along to Io's meadow. He began playing an enchanted tune to send Argus to sleep. It didn't work. But the next day Hermes started chatting to Argus and, it has to be said, our Hermes can be a very boring young man. If boring was an Olympic sport then Hermes would get a winner's laurel every time. He gets it from his father.

Anyway, Hermes gave up playing the pipes and started chatting to Argus. It seems he started telling Argus the history of the pipes . . . and history was the one subject that used to send Argus to sleep in school. One by one the eyes closed and within an hour all his eyes were shut!

Then Hermes drew his sword and lopped off the head of Argus. There was no need for that. It was cruel but, as I say, Hermes takes after his father.

I was furious. I made sure that Io stayed a cow and I arranged for Argus's ghost to pester her every time she tried to sleep.

Zeus was an unhappy little god, I can tell you. Then one evening he came to me and said, "Io . . ."

"You owe what?" I asked.

"Io. Princess Io."

"What about her?" I sniffed.

"I – erm – I turned her into a cow because I wanted to hide her from you," he muttered miserably.

"Did you now?"

"Yes," he sighed. "And I was wondering if you'd mind if I changed her back again?"

"But you'll just go off flirting with her again," I said.

"No, my lovely sparkling ray of moonlight. Never. And I promise I will never look at another woman – or another goddess, as long as . . . as long as time itself."

Call me foolish, call me weak, but I believed him. I also felt a little sorry for Princess Io. It wasn't her fault that my hopeless husband fell in love with her. So I agreed.

Within a week Io was back in her woman's shape and packed off to Egypt out of the way.

Zeus was so happy I felt I could ask him a favour. "For you, my tender-hearted hippopotamus, anything," he said.

"Argus is dead, but I want to save those lovely eyes of his," I said.

"Why not keep them in a glass bottle?" my hideous husband shrugged. "Or whip them all together with buttermilk and eat them. A sort of eyes-cream?" he laughed.

I was tempted to poke one of his little eyes with my long fingernail but I stayed calm. "I want you to place them in the tail of my favourite bird, the peacock. Then, every time the peacock spreads its tail, the world will be reminded of Argus – and the cruel end he came to."

And that's how the peacock came to have so many eyes in its tail, in case you ever wondered.

You may also wonder if Zeus kept his promise to give up chasing other women.

One morning he said, "I'm off to Crete."

"Fishing?" I sighed.

"Fishing," he said.

"Bring us back a fish supper," I told him.

"If I catch anything," he mumbled.

"You'd better," I said.

He packed a handful of ambrosia into a pouch on his belt. As you know, ambrosia is the food of the gods.

"Is that in case you get hungry?" I asked.

"No," he said. "It's bait for the fish."

"Fish eat ambrosia?" I asked, surprised.

Zeus grinned and chuckled, "Of course. That's why it's called the food of the cods."

My mother warned me. I should have listened.

Top Facts 10:

Top 10 victims

1 Name: Semele
Address: Greece
Appearance: Beautiful nymph
Report: Zeus appeared in human form and invited Semele to become his girlfriend. He simply said, "I am Zeus – be my love and I'll grant you one wish!" Hera heard of this and disguised herself as a human and visited Semele. "He's not Zeus!" she said. "Use your wish. Ask him to appear in his glorious god shape! Bet he can't do it." Semele made her wish and Zeus could not refuse. Sadly, a human cannot look at a god. Semele took one look at Zeus who blazed like lightning . . . and she was burned to a frazzle. Pffffzzzzt! (Hera also ordered that Semele's baby should be torn apart by the giants. They did this but Zeus's mother stuck him back together!)
Say to her: Nice sun-tan you have there! *or* That's life . . . Hera today, gone tomorrow!
Don't say: You're the toast of the town.
Comment: No longer a human being – suit someone who likes a baked being.

2 Name: Aphrodite (called Venus by the Romans)

Address: Olympus

Appearance: Beautiful goddess of love

Report: Aphrodite refused to become Zeus's girlfriend so he forced her to marry Hephaestus. Hephaestus was the son of Hera (and possibly Zeus) and he was a blacksmith. He was also very, very ugly and did his work in the middle of a volcano. This did not suit Aphrodite at all. She found other boyfriends and Hephaestus went off like a volcano – he really blew his top!

Say to her: Venus, you're a star.

Don't say: I hear your husband invented central heating?

Comment: Born from the blood of Uranus mixed with the foam of the sea. Suit someone who likes wet people.

3 Name: Echo

Address: Anywhere on Earth

Appearance: Not much to look at. Invisible in fact!

Report: Echo was a chatty nymph. She could talk the hind leg off a kangaroo. Zeus gave her a job: she was to keep his wife chatting while he sneaked off and met his other girlfriends. When Hera discovered the trick she tied Echo's chatty tongue so that all she could do was repeat the last words of someone else's speech. Echo's love, Narcissus, grew tired of this, he left her and broken-hearted Echo shrivelled away. But her spirit still repeats other people's words. Her voice is the Echo you hear in certain places . . . places . . . places . . .

Say to her: Hello! Hello! Hello!

Don't say: Cat got your tongue?

Comment: Suit someone who likes the sound of their own voice.

---

4 Name: Nemesis

Address: No fixed abode

Appearance: Could be almost anything. Quick-change artist – and not just her clothes!

Report: Nemesis was the daughter of Nyx (the night) so she's a bit of a dark horse. Zeus chased her and she didn't want to be caught so she changed shape a few times. When he finally caught up with her he was in the shape of a swan – but she was in the shape of a goose. He gave her a nasty job – seeking out proud human beings and making sure something very nasty happens to teach them a lesson.

Say to her: Birds of a feather flock together.

Don't say: I'm proud to meet you.

Comment: Suit someone who likes a lark.

5 Name: Europa
Address: Crete
Appearance: Beautiful queen
Report: Zeus cheated . . . as usual. He disguised himself as a handsome but gentle bull and went to visit Europa. She climbed on to his back and that's when he charged off with her. Europa clung on to his horns for dear life

and didn't dare jump off. Zeus jumped into the sea and swam to Crete. She was marooned with him, kidnapped by a bull.
Say to her: Beware of the bull!
Don't say: You were conned into going to Crete. The world's first con-crete in fact!
Comment: Gave her name to the continent of Europe . . . not to mention the Eurovision Song Contest. Suit someone who's tone deaf.

6 Name: Danae
Address: The island of Seriphos
Appearance: Beautiful princess
Report: Danae had a fierce father called Acrisius. Someone told him that his grandson would kill him. He thought he'd put a stop to that by locking his only daughter, Danae, in a tower so

that she couldn't meet anyone or have any children. But it takes more than locks to keep Zeus out. He poured himself through the window as a shower of gold. Danae had a child, Perseus and Acrisius sent them both off in a chest to drown. Zeus made sure they landed safely on Seriphos. (Naturally Perseus returned and killed Acrisius – accidentally.)

Say to her: Fancy some swimming lessons?

Don't say: Fancy a game of "Happy Families"?

Comment: Nice lady but watch out for her son!

---

7 Name: Thetis

Address: The sea

Appearance: Sea goddess – or almost anything she wants to be

Report: Zeus loved her but it was said her son would become greater than Zeus. Zeus decided that she'd have to marry a feeble human so their son could easily be defeated. Zeus picked Peleus but Thetis didn't like him. She changed herself into fire, water, a snake, a lion and a cuttlefish but Peleus stuck to her. She was so impressed she married him.

Say to her: You're incredible; first you change your body, then you change your mind!

Don't say: You looked better as a cuttlefish.

Comment: Suit someone who gets bored easily.

8 Name: Leda

Address: Sparta in Greece

Appearance: Beautiful Queen of Sparta

Report: Zeus fell in love with Leda when he saw her bathing in the river. He didn't want to appear as a man and scare her so he appeared as a swan. As a result Leda laid a couple of eggs! A daughter, Helen, grew from one of them. She became the most beautiful woman in the world and the Greeks and Trojans fought the Trojan War over her.

Say to her: Helen takes after her mother.

Don't say: Fancy some scrambled egg?

Comment: Will suit someone who likes to swan around.

9 Name: Alcmene

Address: A palace, somewhere in Greece

Appearance: Beautiful queen

Report: Alcmene was married when Zeus fell in love with her. She refused to have anything to do with him – no kisses and no cuddles. So Zeus cheated – he really, *really* cheated. He changed his shape so he looked exactly like Alcmene's husband! Then he got a kiss *and* a cuddle. When the real husband came home Alcmene got a bit of a shock. Probably thought she was seeing double. Alcmene had a baby and called him Heracles – Zeus's wife was furious and gave Heracles a really tough time. (But that's another story.)

Say to her: Guess who?

Don't say: Two heads are better than one.

Comment: Easily fooled.

10 Name: Metis

Address: Zeus's head

Appearance: A fly

Report: Zeus was in love with Metis. (This will not come as a surprise to you.) Then he heard that any son of Metis's would be greater than Zeus. (This too may sound familiar by now.) Zeus simply turned Metis into a fly . . . and swallowed her. This did not

prevent Metis's child growing – inside Zeus's head! One day he had a terrible headache, he asked the blacksmith Hephaestus to smack him on the head with a hammer. As Zeus's head split his daughter, Athena, popped out, fully-grown and fully-dressed in armour.

Say to her: Bzzzzzzzz!

Don't say: Is that a spider I see heading towards us?

Comment: Suit someone who likes insects. She's cheap to feed and can entertain you by walking upside down on the ceiling.

Legend 9: Aphrodite

One of the top Greek legends is the story of the Trojan War and the trick of the famous wooden horse. It seems that there really *was* a great ten-year war that destroyed Troy at some time in history.

As usual the Greeks manage to blame a woman (or two) for all the troubles in the world. In this case the women are the goddess of love, Aphrodite, and the beautiful queen Helen. Aphrodite must have become really fed up with being blamed for everything . . . war, murder and cruelty and her story is number 9. What would her side of the story have been?

Helen and the horror horses

Paphos Temple
Cyprus

Zeus
Mount Olympus
Greece

Dear Zeus,

It has to be said. I am fed up. They are at it again. Whenever there's trouble they always cry "Blame Aphrodite!" Now there's this silly little war in Troy and they are off again. "Blame Aphrodite!" Well, it's not good enough, I've had enough and I want to set he record straight. I am not to blame.

I've always had a hard life, ever since I was born. I mean to say, I had no mother or father, did I? The blood of old god Ouranos dripped into the sea and made what the Greeks call "aphros" foam. I grew inside the foam and found myself swimming for my life to the island of Cythera. They named me Aphrodite because

26

I came from the foam. How would you like to go through life being called "Frothy"? It's just not fair.

And, of course, I wasn't just beautiful. Oh, no, I just happened to be the most beautiful goddess ever created. So what happened? They were all jealous, weren't they! The men all wanted to marry me and the women all hated me. Of course you couldn't marry me because you were already married to Hera. So what did you do? You made me marry your son. The ugliest, smelliest most clumsy god on Olympus. Hephaestus, a blacksmith. I suppose that was your idea of a joke, was it?

Naturally I had to find other boyfriends. I mean, who wants to be the wife of a man who spends all day in a volcano? Not me. As you know I fancied young Ares, the god of war. We used to meet and have a cuddle every now and then. We never did anybody any harm. But that Helios, the sun, spotted us. What did he do? Did he warn us? No, the sneaky lump of flaming rock went and split on us. He told Hephaestus!

Hephaestus was just as bad. He could have

27

had a quiet word with Ares ... hit him with one of his hammers or something. But, no. Hephaestus has to make me look a right fool. He makes a trap from an invisible metal net and tells me he's off for a party with his mates. When Ares called round to see me the net closed in and we were trapped. You gods all turned up to see Ares and me trapped in the net, didn't you? You all had a good laugh. I have never been so embarrassed in my life.

But the point I'm making is this – it wasn't my fault. It was your fault, Zeus, for making me marry Hephaestus. And it was your fault that Hephaestus was so ugly. Remember? He tried to break up a fight between you and Hera. So what did you do? Threw him out of the window. It took the poor lad nine days to land on Lemnos. Nine days! No wonder he looks a bit rough after he hit the ground. You would be a bit battered if your dad did that to you.

Then there's the story of Adonis. Now that was definitely not my fault. That was that nasty witch Persephone's fault. I might remind you that she's another of your daughters. Nothing

but trouble, your family. Miserable old bat. Not
surprising since she has to spend four months a
year in the Underworld.

Anyway, as I was saying, she fell in love with
Adonis. I can't say I blame her. He was a lovely
lad, even if he was a human. But I saw him first.
I found him as a baby. And I just asked
Persephone to look after him. What did she do?
She tried to steal him. I wasn't having that so I
went to you to sort the argument out. You
decided he'd have four months of the year alone,
four months with Persephone and four months
with me. I wasn't happy but I stuck to the deal.

But your Persephone wasn't satisfied. Oh, no,
she had to go and tell my gentleman friend,
Ares, that I was in love with Adonis! Naturally
he was a bit upset. Naturally he turned himself
into a wild boar, chased after poor little Adonis
and gored him to death. (You can still see the
spot where his blood fell because those nice
anemone flowers grow there.) That crafty witch
Persephone knew that dead Adonis would end
up in the Underworld where she is queen. So I
was glad you brought him back to life and let

him live with me every summer. Still, it was a messy business and, as I said, it was not my fault. But I still get the blame. "There's Aphrodite," they all said. "At it again. Goddess of love, she calls herself. Brings nothing but misery."

The same thing happened with Glaucus. He was a nasty piece of work that Glaucus. He was mad about horses but he took it a little bit too far. He used to feed them on human flesh. This was to build up their strength and make sure they'd win all their races. Everybody else was feeding their horses grass so Glaucus was cheating. All I wanted to do was teach him a bit of a lesson. He had said some very insulting things about me but I'm not bitter. All I did was give his horses water from a magic well and feed them a few sacred herbs.

The next day the horses ran like the wind. The gruesome Glaucus couldn't control them and he fell off. And, of course, his hungry horses smelled the blood and ate him. Every last scrap, bones and all. I say it serves him right. It wasn't my fault, but they all cried, "Blame Aphrodite!" as usual.

Now there's this Trojan War business and I want you to put a stop to the nasty gossip. You know how it all started. It was the goddess of spite Eris who threw that golden apple into a feast we were having on Olympus. Spiteful isn't the word for it. She's even worse than your Persephone. Eris had written, "For the fairest" on the side of the apple. Naturally I thought that was me! Everyone says I'm the most beautiful thing they've ever seen. For some reason your wife Hera thought she should have the apple and then your daughter Athena tried to say she was the fairest. (That, in my opinion, is a joke, but I wouldn't want you to think I'm being bitchy.)

We turned to you, didn't we? We said, "Well, Zeus? Who's the fairest?"

And what did you do? You lost your bottle. You didn't dare tell your wife and daughter that I was more beautiful than them. You said Prince Paris of Troy could judge between us.

What happened next wasn't my fault. Those two ugly crows knew they couldn't beat me so they tried to bribe Prince Paris! Hera offered him

31

power – said he'd be a great ruler – and Athene offered to make him a great fighter. What could poor little Aphrodite do? I offered him the love of the most beautiful human woman on earth, Helen.

Of course Paris gave the golden apple to me. But that was only fair because I am the most beautiful by far. Is it my fault that he won the love of Helen? Was it my fault that Helen was already married? And was it my fault that he stole her from her husband and took her off to Troy?

But they're all blaming me. Now Helen's husband, Menelaus, has raised a huge army and has been attacking Troy for ten years to try and get her back. "Blame Aphrodite!" they're saying.

Well, I'm going to put an end to this war. I have whispered in Odysseus's ear, "Remember Glaucus!" . . . a horse full of human flesh. Now he's going to build a wooden horse and fill it full of soldiers. The Trojans will take the horse into

the city and the soldiers will jump out and massacre them.

That'll put an end to this boring war. The Greeks can go home happy and Menelaus can have his little Helen back. But will they be happy? I'll bet they won't. They'll do what they always do... they'll whinge and moan and look for someone to blame. And we all know who they'll choose!

Yours truly

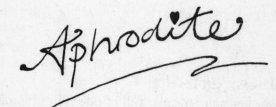

Top Facts 9: Wicked women

Women in the Greek world were told they were second best. They were little better than slaves. So when it came to stories of the gods it was often women who made trouble.

It wasn't just the Greeks who blamed women for bad things in the world. The very first Bible story put Adam and Eve in the garden of Eden. It was the woman Eve who persuaded Adam to eat the apple from the tree of knowledge. Eating the fruit got them thrown out of Paradise and on to Earth with all its wickedness. For thousands of years people believed in this idea – there would be no problems, if it wasn't for women.

Nowadays we can see how unfair this is. But in Greek legends we have lots of examples of weak and wicked women.

1 Pandora
Weakness: curiosity

The word *pandora* means "full of talent" and Pandora was a good housewife, a good talker, rich . . . and evil of course. The blacksmith god Hephaestus made her out of clay and Zeus sent her to Earth as a punishment for men. She was the first woman (like Eve) and Zeus sent her as a gift to Epimetheus. Epimetheus had another gift – a jar that came with an order from Zeus: "Do not open!" Pandora simply couldn't resist it. She took the lid off the jar and out flew all the evils and miseries that we have on Earth: disease, greed, envy, hatred and so on. Before she could slap the lid back on they had escaped and infected the world. Only one good thing remained behind to cheer us up: Hope. We can only "hope" Pandora gets those miseries back in the jar one day!

2 Danaus's daughters
Weakness: murder

Danaus had fifty daughters . . . and forty-nine of them murdered their husbands! He had married his fifty daughters to his brother's fifty sons. Then he got a message saying they would all be killed. He told the girls to kill their husbands first and each of them was given a huge hair pin. Forty-nine stabbed their husbands to death . . . one softy let her husband live so not all women are evil. (Only 49 out of every 50!)

Of course, they didn't get away with it. When they died they went to Tartarus (a place deeper underground than Hades) where they were forced to carry water from one place to another. The trouble is they were given leaky jars so the job would never be completed. They are probably still at it now. (This seems a bit unfair since they were only doing what their dad told them to do!)

3 Ino
Weakness: hatred

Ino was like the wicked stepmother in every fairy tale you have ever heard. She really hated her sweet step-children Phrixus and Helle. First Ino dried all the grain in the grain store so the crops wouldn't grow and the people starved. Her husband Athamas didn't know what to do until he received a message saying he had to make a sacrifice to the gods . . . and the sacrifice was to be Phrixus and Helle! The goddess Hera sent a golden ram to rescue them and, of course, Ino was upset. But not for long. When her husband discovered the truth he forced Ino to jump off a cliff into the sea and drown.

Still Ino had the last laugh. Helle tried to escape on the back of the golden ram as well. As it flew home she fell off into the sea and drowned. Athamas finally made his sacrifice to the gods and he sacrificed the golden ram! This seems a bit unfair on the ram because it wasn't his fault Helle fell off. Later heroes went in search of the fleece of the golden ram . . . but that's another story.

4 Scylla
Weakness: betrayal

Scylla let her dad down badly. He was fighting against Minos, King of Crete, and doing quite well because he had a magic lock of hair. This was a lock of purple hair that grew on his head. Wicked Scylla fell in love with the enemy Minos and gave him the lock of hair after pinching it from her sleeping dad! In the very next battle Scylla's dad was killed. But Scylla didn't end up happy ever after. She expected Minos to love her and marry her . . . in fact he hated her and sailed away from her.

Scylla didn't give up that easily. She started swimming after Minos's boat. She might even have caught him but an eagle appeared and drowned her. Little did she know that the eagle was really the ghost of her dead dad. Revenge is sweet! Scylla was turned into an ugly sea monster – or a lonely, homeless sea-bird like a gull or a tern. One good turn deserves another, they say. Or, in this case, one bad tern.

5 Athene
Weakness: revenge

A dangerous woman if you upset her. One poor fella called Tiresias happened to see her in the bath. She was so upset she blinded him . . . she later felt a little bit sorry and gave him the gift of being able to see into the future. This is not so good as being able to see your dinner, of course.

Women who upset her came off even worse. Arachne said she was a better weaver than Athene. Spiteful Athene turned her into a spider and spiders have been spinning ever since. (They have also suffered a lot from being washed down the plug-hole of the bath!)

Medusa also annoyed Athene and ended up with goggle eyes, a swollen tongue, snakes instead of hair, wings and brass claws. Such an ugly creature that any human who looked at her turned to stone. A hard punishment. Rock hard in fact.

◊ Ariadne
Weakness: cunning

Another daughter who betrayed her father. Ariadne's father, Minos, had a lovely pet Minotaur – a monster with the head of a bull and the body of a man that lived in an underground maze. Unlike a bull it was *not* a vegetarian – it ate people. Ariadne showed the hero, Theseus, how to get out of the maze when he'd killed it – she gave him a thread to trail behind him. Then she gave him a magic sword which was the only thing that would kill the Minotaur.

Ariadne then showed Theseus how to sink her father's ships (by boring holes in the bottom) and she drugged the palace guards and sailed off with him. Ariadne did not live happy ever after – well, not with Theseus. He dropped her on an island and as soon as she fell asleep he sailed off without her! She married a god called Nisus instead. Killing your dad's pet monster is still not a good idea and do not try it at home.

39

7 Clytemnestra
Weakness: temper

Clytemnestra was married to King Agamemnon . . . and she hated him. You can hardly blame her really. She never wanted to marry him in the first place. And, in the second place, he sacrificed their daughter to the gods!

Agamemnon sailed off to fight in the Trojan War for ten years. Clytemnestra didn't forgive or forget. When he came home he even had a new girlfriend. He was really asking for it and he got it. Clytemnestra welcomed him with a feast (which was nice) and by murdering him in his bath (which was not so nice but, as he was in the bath, she didn't get blood over her clean bathroom floor).

Clytemnestra married Agamemnon's brother. (This is called "keeping it in the family".) Then she was eventually murdered by her own son. (This is taking "keeping it in the family" a bit far. Don't try this at home.)

8 Deineira
Weakness: stupidity

Deineira was so beautiful that the hero, Heracles, fell in love with her and married her. A centaur (half-horse, half-man) tried to gallop off with Deineira but Heracles shot him with a poisoned arrow. As the centaur was dying he whispered a secret to Deineira. "Dip a shirt in my blood. If Heracles ever falls in love with someone else then put the shirt on him. You will win him back. Aaaaggggh!" And he died.

Dim-wit Deineira believed the centaur! She thought Heracles fancied an old girlfriend so she begged him to put on the shirt, which he did. Then terrible pains shot through his body as if his blood was boiling. He couldn't get the shirt off because it stuck to him like tar. Even the mighty Heracles couldn't stand the agony. He killed the servant who brought the shirt (very unfair), then tore down trees to build a bonfire. He lay on top of the bonfire and ordered his servants to light it. Zeus rescued him and took him to Olympus.

When Deineira heard the news she was so upset she killed herself. (Sadly Zeus did not rescue her.) This just goes to show, you should never believe anything a dying horse whispers in your ear. You have been warned.

9 Harpies
Weakness: nagging

These delightful creatures have the body of a bird and the head of a woman. They have a job to do. It's a nasty job, but someone has to do it. They fly down and make life a misery for criminals. Their screeching will stop you ever getting to sleep again, they settle on your food and their birdy droppings put you right off eating it, even though you are starving. They smell absolutely terrible and they never give up. They just go on and on, reminding you how wicked you have been. In the end they pick you up and carry you down to Hell. By this time you are probably quite glad to go with them. At least you'll get a decent meal and a good night's sleep.

10 Phaedra
Weakness: jealousy

Another wicked stepmother. She said that her step-son, Hippolytus, had attacked her. This was one whacking great fib. Poor young Hippolytus was out riding in his chariot one day when the avenging sea god, Poseidon, made a huge wave. The horses got the shock of their lives and bolted. Hippolytus was dragged along, bashing his head against boulders (and scraping his knees pretty nastily on the sand) until he died.

Of course Phaedra's fib was found out. She knew she was in trouble so she hanged herself. (Poseidon being a god, and a man, didn't actually suffer any punishment for the murder of Hippolytus.)

Being a woman in Ancient Greece was tough. Being a woman in Greek legends was deadly!

Legend 8: Orpheus and Eurydice*

The Greeks, as you'll have spotted by now, were not very keen on happy endings. They invented the word "tragedy". (Actually the word tragedy comes from two Greek words for "goat" and "song". If you've ever heard a goat trying to sing then you'll understand; you don't get much more tragic than a singing goat.)

If you have a brave warrior then he'll die, tragically, in Greek legend. (If you had a legendary Greek birthday party then the guests would probably be burnt to death when the candles were lit, the cake would fall on the floor and the birthday girl's knickers catch fire!)

And, of course, if you have two lovers then they just have to live miserably ever after. Britain's great playwright William Shakespeare wrote ". . .the course of true love never did run smooth". If he'd been a Greek writer he'd have said ". . . the course of true love has more ups and downs than a bungee jump."

Take top story number 8, Orpheus and Eurydice for example . . .

* Eurydice is pronounced "your-a-dice" in this poem.

If looks could kill

When it came to music
They say Orpheus was the best.
He played the lyre and sang as sweet
As birdies on the nest.

The savage beasts were rocking
And behaved as good as gold.
The stones came from the mountain
Just to hear him. How they rolled!!

His music soothed a dragon
While he stole its golden fleece.
He came back and got married
To his Eurydice in Greece.

But Eury went out walking
And was chased by some cruel god.
She never made it home because
Upon a snake she trod.

Poor Eury dropped down cold
And went down to her death in Hades.
It broke her husband's heart because
He'd loved no other ladies!

But Orpheus was angry
"Oh woe!" he cried, "Alack!
I'll walk right down to Hades
And I'll get my Eury back."

He packed his bags, he packed his lyre,
And set out full of fury.
Crossing mountains, crossing seas,
Just to reach his Eury.

He reached the gates of Hades,
Found it guarded by a dog.
He played his lyre and its three heads
All slept . . . just like a log.

He crossed the poisoned River Styx
And walked down into Hell.
The great god Hades cried,
"A live man! Well! Well Well!"

The god of Hell refused at first
To give up Eurydice.
But Young Orph pulled his lyre out
And sang a song . . . real nice.

So Hades told the singer
"Take your Eury, never mind.
Go back the way you came, my lad,
And she'll be right behind."

But Hades gave a warning,
He said, "You must trust me son.
Don't dare to look round – no not once
Or Eury will be gone."

The couple crossed the river Styx
They walked out past the guard.
Still he looked out straight ahead
Although he found it hard.

They climbed up almost to the top.
The going it was rough.
The singer turned! He saw his wife!
She vanished in a puff!

This loss drove Orpheus off his head.
It also broke his heart.
He picked a fight with some wild women . . .
They tore him apart.

They threw his head into the river
(That was just not nice)
And, as it floated out to sea,
It cried out, "Eurydice!"

End

THERE'S NOTHING LIKE A HAPPY ENDING

YEAH.... AND THIS IS NOTHING LIKE A HAPPY ENDING!!

Top Facts 8: Gruesome Greek life

You may think Orpheus had a gory Greek life but it was not unusual in the gruelling Greek age. Even his lyre was the result of some bloodthirsty butchery.

Here's how the great poet Homer described the first lyre being made. Of course Homer was supposed to be blind, he didn't have to look at the guts and gore all over the floor.

WARNING!

a) Do not try this at home.
b) The following description is not suitable for vegetarians to read.

Top 10 tips for a lyrical lyre

Title: *Make your own lyre*
A Blueus Peterus Guide

You will need:
A tortoise, an ox and a sheep. Wood, a knife (and a mop for the blood).

Method:
1 If the tortoise is alive then kill it.

2 Scoop the insides from the tortoise – the shell will be your sound box.

3 If the ox is alive then kill it. Skin the ox.

4 Wrap the ox hide round the shell. (Keep the ox meat. It will make a good sacrifice to the god Hermes who made the very first lyre this way.)

5 Add wooden "horns" and tuning pegs as shown in picture.

6 If the sheep is alive then kill it. (Don't forget to wash your hands when you have finished all this killing.)

7 Take out the sheep's guts and clean them.

8 Dry the guts in the sun. (Your mum can have the rest of the sheep to make shepherd's pie.)

9 Stretch seven strings of sheep gut across the shell and on to the tuning pegs.

10 Pluck the strings with your fingers to make a sound. You will be turtle-y amazed!

Grim Greece

Life . . . and death . . . could be hard for tortoises. It could also be grim for the Greeks. The Greeks enjoyed music. We know a little bit about their instruments because remains have been found in graves. We know a little about their songs because they were written down. We have very little idea of how Greek music might have sounded though.

Music had its own god, Hermes. This god who came across a tortoise eating grass, strangled the creature and made it into the world's first lyre. The Greeks usually had a god to look after different parts of their lives. If Greek life was cruel then it's no surprise that the gods and goddesses were so cruel.

Did you know . . . ?

1 Potty punishments Many of the Greeks lived in cities and the greatest punishment for a criminal was to be thrown out of the city. Exiled. In Athens the freeborn men of the city could vote in a sort of parliament – but not women, slaves, foreigners or men under 30. These voters would be given a piece of broken pottery. They would scratch the name of someone they wanted thrown out. The name that appeared most was sent out of the city. The exile would probably die outside the safety of the city. Inside the city of Athens you were protected by walls, by laws and, of course, by the goddess Athena.

2 Sickly sacrifices Big religious ceremonies took place outside Greek temples where sacrifices were made to the god of that temple. Cattle, sheep, goats or pigs would be led in front of the open doors – this was so the god could look out and see the sacrifice. The animal would be decorated with flowers and its horns covered in gold. The priest would cut the animal's throat, part of it would be burnt on the altar as a gift to the god. The rest would be roasted and eaten by the Greeks. The priests usually got the best bits – the gods often got the parts not worth eating! The Greeks would make a sacrifice to a goddess like Demeter, the goddess of grain, so she would give them a rich harvest.

3 Grave games The Olympic games were held once every four years in honour of Zeus. But they were so dangerous they would be banned today! A wrestling-boxing game called pankration allowed anything except biting or gouging finger's into your opponent's eyes. Contestants could die in this sport. So could chariot racers if drivers fell off or overturned. And the spectators (men only) weren't too comfortable either. A writer called Epicetus wrote, *"Aren't you scorched by the fierce heat and crushed by the crowd? Aren't you soaked by the rain and deafened by the noise? And don't you suffer all that for the excitement of the games?"*

4 Painful parties The rich Greeks enjoyed being entertained at home. But even that wasn't safe for everyone. A woman dancer would perform on the floor. Then a hoop would be brought in. Swords were set in the hoop with the points upwards. The dancer would do somersaults over the swords, into the middle of the hoop then out again. One slip and she was impaled on the tip of a sword. Athena was goddess of Athens and goddess of the arts – she would protect the dancers. Guests could suffer too. One game involved solving riddles. If someone failed to solve the riddle then they had to drink a goblet of wine with salt in! Dionysus, god of wine, might not have approved!

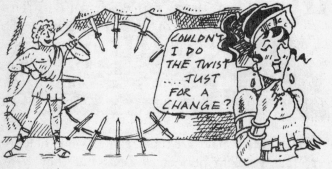

COULDN'T I DO THE TWIST ....JUST FOR A CHANGE?

5 Foul fights Greeks enjoyed hunting and killing animals. They also liked to watch animals killing each other. Dog fights and cock fights were common in the Greek age. The spectators would enjoy the bloodshed and they would also enjoy betting on which animal would win. They even enjoyed watching fighting cats! Artemis, the goddess of hunting, would enjoy this cruelty to animals. The Greeks believed. As goddess of the Moon she looks down on you from her silver chariot pulled by stags.

6 Suffering slaves Rich Greeks lived quite comfortably but only because they had slaves to do all the dirty work. Some slaves were very clever and they taught the children of their masters. Others suffered a dreadful life of back-breaking work and terrible food in the silver mines of Laurion. They dug out the silver for coins – but never received any payment except an early death. There was always a chance that the gods of the Underworld, Hades and his wife Persephone, might take care of them. They certainly had no god to help them on Earth!

7 Peculiar predictions The Greeks liked to know what would happen in the future . . . just as many people do today. In modern times there are palm-readers in fairgrounds, readers of Tarot Cards over the telephone and, most popular, horoscope writers in newspapers. The Greeks also had lots of ways of predicting the future – from dreams and claps of thunder to sneezes! But most popular was to talk to the gods and hear what they had to say. The gods spoke through human priests known as "oracles". At Zeus's temple in Dodona the priests listened to the wind rustling leaves in the oak trees – others examined the liver of a freshly-slaughtered animal. But most famous was the Oracle at Delphi where an old woman sat half-asleep and muttered weird words. The priests would tell you what she meant – if you paid them! The Oracle was never "wrong" – the people of Athens were told to take their army to Sicily in 415 BC. The army was massacred. The priests said, "Zeus meant take them to Sicily – a small hill of that name near Athens!"

8 Horrible hunting Hunting was so important it had its

own goddess, Artemis. Before a hunter set out he would have to promise to give some of the catch to Artemis. (Why couldn't she just go and catch her own?) Men hunted alone, with a few slaves or a couple of friends, but not in large groups. Hares were the most common animal to be hunted. The hunters would lay out nets and use dogs to drive the hares into the nets. Deer would be hunted on horseback and the hunters would try to slow the deer by catching their feet in traps then finishing them off with javelins and clubs. Hunting boar was the most dangerous thing because the boars could fight back! A Greek book on hunting warned that if a boar knocked your spear from your hand then you should lie down flat and cling to the grass – with any luck it couldn't get its sharp tusks under you to gore you. While you were down there it wouldn't do any harm to say a few prayers to Artemis!

9 Foul funerals A dead person had to be prepared for the trip to the Underworld before they were buried. They'd be wrapped in everyday clothes and a small coin was placed in the mouth. This would be used to pay Charon, a ferryman, to row you over the River Styx into the land of the god Hades. The corpse would also be given a piece of cake. That would feed the guard dog Cerberus. (Of course, Cerberus had three heads so three pieces of cake would have been better!) A woman would be expected to wail, beat her head and tear out her hair as her husband lay dead. The body would be carried to the burial place before dawn because Apollo's sun should not look down on the dead. The body would be placed in the ground and the mourners go home to a feast.

10 Brutal birth The goddess Hera looked after women during the birth of a child. But there was no god or goddess for the children themselves. In fact children could be treated quite brutally. Girls were unpopular in many Greek towns or villages. They ate the family food then had to be given a large present when they married. Weak or sick babies would also be wasteful – if they didn't grow up strong then they couldn't help to work in the fields and provide for themselves. For the first ten days of a baby's life the father could decide if it lived or died. If it was not wanted (because it was another girl or a sickly weakling) then it was put in a cradle and left in a public place. A rejected child might be picked up by kindly family – if it was lucky. An unlucky one would be left to die.

Legend 7: Perseus and Medusa

The Greek gods could be cruel or funny or kindly or evil. But they couldn't really be heroes and heroines. After all, they were "immortal" – they could not be killed. It's easy to do daring deeds when you know you are going to live.

Even *you* would save a jelly baby from the path of an oncoming steamroller if you knew the steamroller was going to bounce off you.

So when the Greeks wanted heroes and heroines they had to have *humans*. Some of these heroes had a god or goddess for one parent. That helped a bit but they could still die doing daringly dreadful and dangerous deeds.

Perseus is a good example and his story makes it to number 7 in the top 10. His father was Zeus and his mother the human Danae. Danae's father, Acrisius, was told his grandson must kill him. So, when grandson Perseus was born, Acrisius dumped the baby and Danae in a wooden chest and threw them into the sea. Of course, they survived and Perseus grew up with Dictys, King Polydectes' brother. But his troubles had only just started . . .

60

Monstrous Medusa and my mum.

Day 1

My mum says I'm going to be a hero.
"Perseus!" she says, "you are going to be
your mum's little hero."

"Thanks, mum," I said.

Course it's hard being a hero here.
That King Polydectes thinks he's the
greatest man in the Kingdom. Smarmy
little creep. And that King Polydectes
fancies my mum. Well, he'd better
just keep off her while I'm around.
My mum's my mum and nobody
else is going to get her. So there.
MUM Course I won't be around to look
after her for a little while. I'm going
away. I don't know quite how that
happened to tell you the truth.

It all started when King Polydectes
said he was going to marry some
princess called Hippodamia. That made a
change from him saying he was going
to marry my mum! He asked
everyone to give him a gift and
they all promised to give him a
horse. Now my mum doesn't give me
no pocket money. So I says, "I'll give you
anything you want .... even one
gorgon's head."

And King Polydectes grinned and said
"Right, Son, you're on!"

And I sort of dropped myself in it. Cos as
you know, the Gorgon's head is so ugly it

"...turns people to stone just to look at it. It's a bit hard cutting somebody's head off when you're a statue, isn't it? And it's even harder cutting somebody's head off if you've got your eyes closed. I tried cutting an apple with my eyes closed and I just cut my finger instead. It didn't half hurt."

Anyway, my mum says my dad, Zeus, is bound to send some help and he's dead powerful, my dad. I just wish he had the power to stop me being seasick cos if he doesn't I'm going to throw up all over this here diary! Oooooops! Here I g..............

Day 27

My mum was right. Who did I meet today but a goddess! "Hello, pet," she said. "I'm your Auntie Athene."

I said, "Hello Auntie Athene, pleased to meet you. I'm on my way to kill the Gorgon."

AUNTIE ATHENE

"I know, pet," she said, "I'm the goddess of wisdom so I know everything. And it was your Auntie Athene that turned Medusa into a Gorgon for carrying on in my temple."

Then Auntie Athene showed me a picture of this monster with boar's tusks for teeth, brass claws for hands, a tongue like a melon and snakes where her hair should be.

Ugly! Hey she was nearly as ugly as King Polydectes, and that's saying something.

Auntie Athene said I hadn't got to look at Medusa but I <u>could</u> look

62

at her if I looked in a mirror. I asked her where I could get one - cos there were no shops in the middle of the sea — and she said she just happened to have one. It was a shield polished so bright you could see your reflection in it.

Then I met another member of the family, my cousin Hermes, and he gave me a sword in the shape of a sickle. (And talking about sickles you'll be pleased to know I stopped being sea-sickle after a week or two.)

Cousin Hermes said I needed a pair of sandals with wings on so I could get away quickly. He said I needed a cloak to make me invisible and a magic sack to carry the head of Medusa after I'd cut it off. I said "Where do I get those things from?" and he said "From the Stygian Nymphs." And I said "Where will I find them?" and he said, "I don't know." And I said "That's not much use then!" but my Auntie Athene said I should ask the Gorgon's sisters, the grey ones.

So that's where I'm off to now

Day 37

I've met the grey ones. THE GREY ONES I don't know why they're called that so don't ask me. They are three women... ..... and they have grey hair. But they only have one eye

...and one tooth between them. "Where can I find the Stygian Nymphs and your sister, Medusa?" and the Grey Ones said "Push off and mind your own business!"

That's no way to speak to a hero, is it? "I'll kill the lot of you!" I said. "I've got a special sword." I said. "If you kill us then you'll never find the Stygian Nymphs or our Medusa, will you?" one of them said. She had a point. Then one of them said "Give me the eye. I want to look at this cheeky little hero." That's when I saw my chance. As one took the eye out and passed it across I snatched the eye off her. Then the one with the tooth took it out to polish it and I snatched that off her, too. "Right, Grey Ones. I've got your eye and your tooth. Tell me what I want to know or you'll not see tomorrow...... and you'll never eat lunch in this town again."

They called me a few very nasty names, I can tell you. I was SHOCKED! But, in the end, they told me what I wanted to know.

"Now can we have our eye back?" one of the Grey Ones asked.

"And our tooth? I'm desperate for me dinner."

You understand, I'm a <u>HERO</u>. Brave in defeat, generous in victory, friend of the poor and enemy of evil. So I said "<u>NO</u>".

Now I'm off to find the Stygian Nymphs."

Day 61

The good news is Medusa doesn't have a snake covered head any longer. I've got it. In a goatskin bag here.

I got the winged sandals, the cloak of invisibility and this bag and I put the sandals on. Its amazing. I just soared up into the air like a bird. Mind you, it's just as well humans can't fly. If they could then they'd discover something more horrible than sea-sickness. It's air-sickness. I brought my dinner up over the Aegean Sea. But I'm a hero, so I'm not complaining.

When I reached the gorgon's den I was a bit shocked to see stone statues all around the garden. "Hello," I thought "Some sculptor's been a bit busy here!" And then I realised. They weren't STATUES ..... they were HUMANS that had been turned to stone. Horrible! Men, women, children and tax collectors.

I expected to come face to face with the monstrous Medusa the minute I walked in the door. But I heard a roaring snore and realised she was having a nap. A true hero would have woken her and challenged her to a fair fight. I decided I would cut off her head first and then challenge her to a fight.

I looked at her in my mirror shield, crept up behind her and brought down the sickle sword "Eeee! The sword went through her neck. Pop-pop-pop-pop-pop-pop!

The snakes exploded as they hit the floor. And SHLURRRRRP! The blood dripped as I popped the head into the goat skin sack. "My mum would be proud of her little hero," I said and I jumped up in the air.

It was hard work trying to hold that shield and the sword and the big head in a bag. I decided to stop off in North Africa for a rest in the garden of Atlas. "Hello, great Uncle Atlas!" I said.

"Get lost," he snarled. "Can't you see I'm busy?"

"Doing what?" I said. "Holding the sky up on me back," He said. "Want to hold it for a minute, sonny?"

"Nah," I said. "I've heard the story about how you tried to trick Heracles into taking the job. It's your punishment so you have to take it like a man."

"I'm not a man," he growled. "I'm a god."

"Yeah, whatever. Just give me one of your golden apples," I said "I'm a hero and I need a break."

"Then break your neck," he said. He was very nasty to me.

"Give me an apple or else," I said "Or else what?" he said.

I just closed my eyes, opened the bag. took out the head and waved it in front of him. After half a minute I popped the head back. opened my eyes and looked at him. The giant was solid stone. If you don't believe me you can go and see him now. He's a mountain. I think the local "people call the mountain "Atlas.""

Just goes to prove. You don't mess with Perseus — even if you are a god.

Off home now. 〰〰〰〰〰〰〰〰〰〰〰

Day 87 I'm coming home with something even better than the Gorgon's head. A wife! Her name is Andromeda. I was just flying round the coast of Philistia when I saw this girl. She was chained to a rock. Well, to be honest I didn't notice the chains at first. You see, she had no clothes on and I thought she was just sunbathing. Well, I didn't look too close. You see, because my mum says it's rude to look at ladies with no clothes on.

Anyway I'm just about to fly past when she shouts, "Hey! Are you not going to save us?"

So I stopped and flew down. Well I didn't know where to look. "What do you want me to do, love?"

"There's a terrible sea monster that's terrorising our country." she said. "My mum and dad have put me here as a sacrifice to get rid of it."

"What do you want me to do? Set you free?"

"No. Stupid, I want you to kill the monster." she said.

"All right, love," I said. "Where is it?"

"It'll be along for its dinner in a minute." So I waited with this really nice looking girl, Andromeda. I didn't know where to look so I looked out to sea. "I was thinking..." I said.

"Not many heroes do thinking." she said, sarcastic like.

ANDROMEDA

"I was thinking. If we both get out of this alive, would you fancy

67

marrying me?"

"Have you got pots of money?" she said.

"No, but I've got the Gorgon's head," I said.

"Give us a look," she said.

I was just reaching into the bag to get the head when there was this great roar and a big splash and this sea monster appeared. Well it had no chance against me and my sickle sword. SNIP-SNAP! PLOP! And that was the end of it.

I set Andromeda free and asked her parents if I could marry her.

They said "NO," and sent an army to kill me. I turned the lot of them to stone.

I told you, no one messes with Perseus, didn't I?

Now I'm flying home – flying very low cos I had a heavy enough load before and Andromeda's a big lass.

Day 100 At last me and Andromeda are ready to settle down. But we weren't welcome back into King Polydectes' court, as you can imagine.

"You're still alive," he said.

"looks like it," I said

"Pity," he said.

"I got your present," I said.

"You never!" he said.

"I did," I said.

"I don't believe you. Give us a look!" he said.

"Here you are," I said

"That's not Medusa's heaaaaa......" he started to say and he never said any more. He was stone dead. In fact he was...... STONE!

I went and found my mum. "Hello, mum." I said. "This is Andromeda."

"Pleased to meet you." mum said.

"Nice place you have here," Andromeda said.

"Not as nice as my homeland," mum said.

"So why aren't you living there?" Andromeda asked and my mum told her the story about how it was forecast that I'd kill my granddad.

"Get away!" Andromeda laughed. "The great lummock wouldn't harm a fly — he might murder a monster, turn a god to stone, freeze the blood of an army and kill off a king .... but he wouldn't harm a fly. So let's go home."

So we set off for mum's homeland and we found there was a contest going on. A sports contest. "You'll do well in those, Percy," Andromeda said —— She always called me Percy.

So I entered the contest and started off throwing the discus. Well, the wind just caught this big stone discus

69

"and blew it off the course. It went straight into the stands where the royal family were watching.

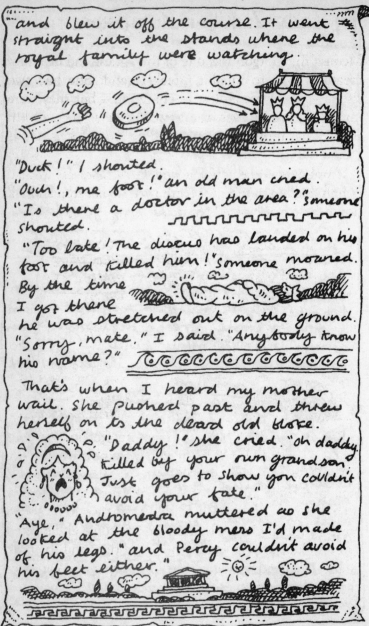

"Duck!" I shouted.

"Ouch!, me foot!" an old man cried.

"Is there a doctor in the area?" someone shouted.

"Too late! The discus has landed on his foot and killed him!" someone moaned. By the time I got there he was stretched out on the ground.

"Sorry, mate." I said. "Anybody know his name?"

That's when I heard my mother wail. She pushed past and threw herself on to the dead old bloke.

"Daddy!" she cried. "Oh daddy. Killed by your own grandson. Just goes to show you couldn't avoid your fate."

"Aye." Andromeda muttered as she looked at the bloody mess I'd made of his legs. "and Percy couldn't avoid his feet either."

Top Facts 7: Killer Creatures

Medusa the Gorgon was one of the ugliest and deadliest creatures ever to inhabit Greek legend. She had two sisters – who were almost as charming – but they were immortal, so not even the power of Perseus could kill them. That means they must still be around somewhere today!

If you ever come across a woman with snakes instead of hair and boars' tusks for teeth then do *not* stop and ask her if she's ever fancied plastic surgery.

Run . . . but don't harm the creature. Report it to your nearest Council Dog Warden who will know what to do.

What we need are sensible, caring people who will look after these killer creatures. The Greeks tried to slay them . . . in the modern, caring world we must try to preserve them. Otherwise they may become endangered species like the blue whale, the white tiger and the pink giraffe. We need wanted adverts for people who can offer caring, sharing homes to these sad, confused creatures. These could be the top 10 adverts . . .

Creature 1 Cerberus

- **Features:** Sits at the entrance to the Underworld. It allows the dead to enter but it doesn't let them out again. If a living person tries to enter then it will eat them. Without this creature we would be overrun with ghosts!
- **Pet control:** Sibyl of Cumae, with Aeneas, fed it a honeyed wheat cake with a sleeping drug mixed in. (If you haven't got a honeyed wheat cake you could try a tin of Pedigree Dead-horse Dog Food.) Orpheus tamed it with sweet music.
- **Reward:** A wonderful guard dog that comes with a year's supply of Pedigree Dead-horse Dog Food.

Creature 2 The Chimera

- **Features:** Breathes fire and eats any champion who sets out to kill it. (Some people believe the Chimera is in fact a volcano – with lions living at the top, goats in the middle and snakes at the base. That's how it breathes fire.)
- **Pet control:** Like King Kong it can be hurt if attacked from the air – the hero Bellepheron rode on Pegasus, the horse with wings. If you haven't got a helicopter or a winged horse then you could try attacking with a fire extinguisher.
- **Reward:** As long as you own it your local water board will give you all the water you need. You'll will never have to suffer a hose-pipe ban.

Creature 3 The Harpies

- **Features:** Harpy means "snatcher". It can snatch a human and carry them off to the Underworld. They can also snatch things from you – they snatched food from blind Phineas as soon as it was put on his table. (He deserved it – he'd put his son's eyes out.)
- **Pet control:** Not so tough as other monsters and can be driven off by a brave person who stands up to them (and wears a clothes peg on the nose). Harpies have never been known to carry off an elephant. You could chain yourself to the nearest elephant and let them try to take you.
- **Reward:** A free bottle of Harpy perfume to keep your enemies away, not to mention your friends!

Creature 4 The Minotaur

- **Features:** A bit of a bully. Will gore and eat anyone who comes too near. When it lived on Crete it was fed on seven young men and seven young women every nine years. As you know bulls are usually vegetarian but the Minotaur enjoyed this snack.
- **Pet control:** The Minotaur was kept in a maze. The fourteen walking dinners could get into the clever maze – but they couldn't get out. Luckily the Minotaur couldn't get out either! Can be harmed by a charmed sword if you happen to have one handy like the hero Theseus had.
- **Reward:** The new owner can keep all the bull's manure to spread on your rhubarb. (No jokes like, "I prefer custard on my rhubarb," please!)

73

Creature 5 The Python

- **Features:** Goddess Hera loaned out the Python to her friends. It can give very good lessons in wickedness.
- **Pet control:** Was badly hurt by Apollo when he shot it full of arrows. A muzzle over that big mouth is a sensible safety precaution.
- **Reward:** You will never be bothered by sales-people selling double-glazing or the milk man demanding his money if you keep this creature in your front garden.

Creature 6 The Typhon

- **Features:** It can speak with the voice of a god, howl like a beast and shoot fire from its eyebrows. Even the gods were so scared they disguised themselves as animals and ran away to Egypt.
- **Pet control:** Zeus had the answer. He kept it under control by using thunderbolts which fried its heads off. If you don't have thunderbolts then buy some nuclear missiles. The Typhon ended up in the sea where it can still stir up the storms named after it – typhoons.
- **Reward:** Use the fire from its eyebrows to cook and heat your house. Save a fortune on gas bills.

Creature 7 The Sphinx

- **Features:** Found on the road to Thebes. It stops passers-by and asks them a riddle. If they get the answer wrong then the Sphinx will eat them. If a passer-by ever got the answer right then the Sphinx would die.
- **Pet control:** Tell it to ask you a question that you already know the answer to! For example: "What's black and white and red all over?" Answer: "An embarrassed penguin."
- **Reward:** Take it into school and say to an unpopular teacher, "So you think you have all the answers, eh . . . .?"

Creature 8 Centaurs

- **Features:** Centaurs are a noisy, drunken gang of bullies, galloping round, kidnapping women. They can be very tricky and tell whacking great lies. It was a centaur whose trickery killed off the mighty Heracles.
- **Pet control:** Poisoned arrows work well to keep them in order. Centaurs teach riding; they will make lovely Pony Club animals so long as you don't let them go to the nearest pub.
- **Reward:** Very useful for pulling a plough, a barge or a lawnmower. Buy a centaur, sell the family car and save a fortune on petrol.

Creature 9 Sirens

- **Features:** Wonderful singing voices that human beings cannot resist. They sing so beautifully that sailors passing their island try to get closer, where their ships are wrecked on sharp rocks and the sailors drown.

- **Pet control:** The explorer Odysseus had himself tied to a mast so he could hear the singing yet not be destroyed. He had his sailors ears plugged with wax so they sailed past without hearing a thing. Keep a good supply of cotton wool handy for stuffing into your ears. Never go near them while you are sailing a boat . . . or riding a bike.
- **Reward:** Great at parties. They'll keep your guests amused all night. In fact you may have trouble getting your guests to ever go home!

Creature 10 The Furies

- **Features:** They are sent by the gods to punish the guilty. They never give up till the terrified criminal has been punished – or executed.
- **Pet control:** They are no trouble at all if you are innocent. If you have any guilty secrets then they'll know about them. It's probably best not to give them a home if you have ever snatched a dummy from a baby or lied to a teacher about your missing homework.
- **Reward:** You'll never be troubled by burglars. They'll know who did it and lead you to the guilty villains. You could even set up as a private detective. With their help they'd solve every case!

Legend 6: Theseus and the Minotaur

The stories of the gods were invented to explain the wonders of nature. How does the sun cross the sky? It sits in a chariot and it's pulled by flying horses, of course. Why does the nightingale sing? Because it was a young woman who was changed into a bird to escape being murdered – the nightingale song is her unhappy tale.

But some of the stories are about people who probably lived in Greece. They are about battles that really happened. Over the years the stories about these real people have had a lot added to them. Take the story of Theseus; he may really have been a powerful king of Athens and won some great battles – that's possible. But the story tellers had him trotting down to the Underworld, and rescuing a goddess – that's unlikely.

The stories say that when Theseus left his mother to meet his father, Aegeus the King of Athens, he chose to walk. On the way he killed a wild sow, a couple of murdering robbers and a giant or two before his father saved him from being poisoned by Medea. All in a day's work for the average hero.

The great enemy of Athens was the island of Crete. After a bitter war, Minos, the King of Crete demanded that Athens send seven young men and seven young women as hostages. That could all be true. It makes sense – so long as Athens stayed at peace then the fourteen hostages would be safe. But this wasn't exciting enough for the story tellers; they said that the unlucky fourteen were *not* hostages, but *sacrifices*! When they reached Crete they would be eaten by a monster!

Sadly, there were no newspapers in ancient Athens. If there had been then they could have had a great time reporting the adventures of Theseus! His story is number 6 in the top 10 . . .

Butchering the bull
Theseus's first task was to free the Athenian people of the terror of the sacrifices to Crete. There was only one thing for it. Theseus had to go himself and sort out the bullying beefsteak . . .

ATHENS ECHO

Hero Thezza to Risk Royal Neck!

Athenian hero, Prince Theseus (known to his adoring people as Thezza) has announced that he will deal personally with the Cretan cretins. Every nine years the city has been sending seven brave boys and seven gallant girls to a dreadful death in Crete – to be eaten by the monstrous Minotaur, – half bull, half man and all powerful. This was the peace treaty forced on the city by the cut-throat Cretan king, Mad Minos.

As panicking parents wondered if their loved one would be selected this time around, hero Thezza (21) announced, "I go!" In a press conference at the palace of his father Aegeus, Thezza told reporters, "Let's see him beat me. I'll kill him. I like killing. I've been practising bull-fighting with my dad's cows. Killed the lot of them. I'm going to grasp the bull by the horns. I'm going to give the Minotaur a taste of my sword."

As reporters ate free beef pies, King Aegeus (62) said, "I'm proud of young Theseus. He didn't have to go and get gored, but he will. It is a far, far better thing he does now than he has ever done before."

The hero and the other thirteen leave at dawn tomorrow on a Sunny Tours cruise ship headed for Crete. The prince says he'll be travelling tourist class with the other sacrificial victims. "I'm no snob," he said. "We're all in this together." The ship will stop at Milos Island for a spot of sight-seeing and is due to arrive in Crete next Tuesday.

Crowds are expected to gather to see the fab fourteen set off. Thezza's ship will be powered by special black sails – in memory of the victims already eaten by the Minotaur. "When he returns he'll change them to white sails," King Aegeus explained. "That will be a sign that the gallant guys and gals have survived."

The Athens Echo will have a reporter on board and hopes to bring you the news within a week of it happening. Remember . . . you read it first in *The Athens Echo*!

Prince Charming!

Prince Theseus of Athens has had a major breakthrough in his battle to beat the Minotaur in Crete . . . and he didn't even have to touch his sword. The handsome, hunky charmer has won the heart of the Cretan king's daughter and plans to use her knowledge to save his comrades.

Last month Prince Theseus (known to his fans as Thezza) set sail with thirteen companions and your *Athens Echo* reporter to the enemy island of Crete, where there's a huge, dark maze of endless, twisting corridors known as the Labyrinth. It was designed by super-inventor Daedalus. At the heart of this maze lurks the beastly bull-man Minotaur. No one who enters the Labyrinth is ever seen again. Thezza and the thirteen are due to be thrown to the Minotaur tomorrow.

Just to be extra cruel, King Minos of Crete holds a party for the victims before they face this dark death. But this time mad Minos has made a serious mistake. Thezza appeared at last night's party and won the heart of Minos's daughter, the lovely Princess Ariadne. Secret talks between the loving couple were overheard only by your *Athens Echo* reporter. He has revealed that tomorrow Prince Perfect will enter the maze with a ball of unbreakable thread. No, he won't use it to strangle the Minotaur, he'll use it to leave a trail back to the entrance.

As soon as the result of the contest is known, your reporter will send news back to Athens on the next boat. Princess Ariadne (19), wearing a white, knee-length chiton with gold and purple edging, told our reporter, "Dad would kill me if he knew what I'd done. But I just love that Prince Theseus. He's such a gentleman. You'd never think he'd killed so many people. And he has dreamy eyes. I'm a sucker for brown eyes. We are planning to marry once he gets out of the Labyrinth."

Meanwhile the noble

sword, a shield or even a bent paper clip to defend myself. Just my bare hands. If I was a betting man then my money would be on the Minotaur."

When he was asked about his relationship with Princess Ariadne he replied, "No comment."

Despite his cautious words your reporter is backing

prince said, "Everybody thinks I'm going to mash the Minotaur and save them. They are forgetting that the Cretans won't let me take a

Thezza to beat the bull and sail back with those white sails blowing in the wind and a new bride by his side.

Thezza triumphs

The bully of Crete is dead! Prince Theseus of Athens has defeated the legendary bull-man of the enemy island and lived to tell the tale. In an interview our hero said, "It's one of the toughest fights I've ever been in. That Minotaur was strong as a bull. Well, you'd expect that, him being a bull and all."

Asked to describe the fight, Thezza said modestly, "I went in to the Labyrinth first. I seemed to walk for miles till I came to this massive monster in the middle. My feet were killing me. The smell was enough to suffocate a super-man. Anyway he came for me with his head down and I grabbed him by the horns. After a couple of hours of struggling I could tell he was getting tired. That's when I gave a sharp twist and heard his neck snap. He gave a bellow, fell to the floor and died."

The prince sipped spiced wine from a gold cup as he described the long journey back. "Just as well I had a thread to help me. That place was an absolute maze."

Princess Ariadne of Crete fed Thezza sweetmeats as he talked. She sat on the arm of his chair in her pale-blue, mini-length chiton with silver brooches at the shoulders. When asked about their wedding plans Ariadne blushed prettily while Thezza said, "No comment."

Reports came in that a furious King Minos of Crete (49) was coming to massacre Theseus and his thirteen friends. They fled to the Athens ship with Princess Ariadne joining them. Your reporter caught the next boat back. It is understood the happy couple will stop off at Naxos for a honeymoon before coming back to a hero's welcome in Athens next week.

Thezza Homecoming Shock

Prince Theseus is back. Crowds gathered on the headland overlooking the sea and cheered as his black-sailed ship sped into harbour. Thezza stood in the prow and waved to his adoring fans. But the question on everyone's lips was, "Where's Princess Ariadne?"

An *Athens Echo* reporter met one of the sailors in a tavern and after several jars of wine the sailor revealed the full story. "We stopped off at Naxos," he said. "Very keen to stop off at Naxos was young Thez. Anyway, the prince got off the boat with young Ariadne, – lovely girl – pale yellow chiton down to her calves, decorated with gold brooches . . . the chiton not the calves. Anyway, he starts talking to her. Telling her all about his great victories. Before you know it she drops off to sleep. Well, you can't blame the girl. Thezza's a great fighter but when it comes to "boring" he could be Olympic Champion! Anyway, as I say, she drops off to sleep, Thezza jumps up and paddles back out to the ship. "Right lads. Up anchor and let's get the Hades out of here!" he cries. Well, we looked at each other a bit funny like. But nobody wanted to upset the Prince and ask him about the Princess snoring on the beach. So we just sailed away and left her there."

The sailor was unable to say why Prince Theseus abandoned Princess Ariadne. It's a mystery.

An official banquet will be held at the temple of Athene tomorrow to celebrate his homecoming. Theseus has been asked to break a bull's neck and sacrifice it to the goddess.

Late extra: King Crash Shock

King Aegeus is dead! As his son Theseus returned after his greatest victory, the old king fell to his death. Athens is in mourning and tomorrow's sacrifice has been cancelled.

It seems King Aegeus heard that his son's ship was returning and he followed the crowds to the headland to watch. Sure enough the vessel appeared on the horizon. "He left with black sails and he will return with white!" the old man predicted.

agreement we had. If he killed the Minotaur, and came home safely, then he'd fit the white sails! Look for yourself. What colour are those sails?"

"They're black, your majesty," the minister muttered.

"What?" the old man cried. His sight has been failing for some time now. But five minutes later the ship was close enough for even King Aegeus to see the black sails. "He's dead!" the old man wailed. He took a step towards the edge of the

After five minutes one of his ministers was given the job of approaching the king and asking, "Why do you say he should have white sails?"

King Aegeus explained impatiently, "It was an

headland, just a pace or two from the steep cliff. "Dead! " he cried and stepped forward. "Dead!" he cried and took another step forward. "Deaaaaaaa. . .ggggh" he cried as he tumbled over the cliff.

Doctors rushed to the bottom to tend to him. The old man looked up. The doctor said, "I have some good news and some bad news, your majesty."

"What's the good news?" the king gasped.

"Prince Theseus is alive and well and has just landed. He's heard about your fall, your majesty. He's on his way to see you. He's been delayed signing autographs."

"But why didn't he change the sails from black to white?" the king croaked.

"Says he forgot, your majesty."

"Silly little beggar," Aegeus moaned. "So what's the bad news?"

"Your neck's broken and you'll be dead before he gets here, your majesty."

"That's a nuisance," King Aegeus sighed. They were to be his last words.

New King Theseus was said to be extremely upset by the death of his father. "I've always had a wonderful memory," he said sadly.

Asked if he would carry on where King Aegeus left off, Theseus replied, "King who?"

The coronation will be held as soon as the crown has been straightened by the jewellers.

King Aegeus is dead . . . *The Athens Echo* says, Gods save King Theseus!

Did you know . . . ?
None of the old legends really explains why Theseus dumped Ariadne on Naxos. Maybe the clue is in what happened next . . . he forgot to change the sails. Maybe that's the answer! He went ashore with Ariadne . . . and *forgot* her! A three thousand year old mystery solved!

Top Facts 6: The legendary world

The Greeks had some very clever scientists. In 300 BC they knew the world was not flat but a globe. They even worked out how large the Earth was and they were very close to getting it right.

An explorer called Pytheas sailed to Britain, gave the British Isles their name, then sailed further and reached the Arctic Circle. When he returned a lot of Greek geographers called him a liar. They preferred to believe the old Greek ideas about Earth. The ideas that might be explained by Zeus as follows . . .

"I am Zeus and the greatest god in the Greek heaven. But I wouldn't want you to think that I *created* these worlds because I didn't. No, that was done by my granny, Mother Earth. You are probably standing on her right now, so just show some respect.

Now Mother Earth is huge and her clothes are grass and trees and rivers and seas. So, with a huge mother like that, you can see why her children were giants. Her husband was Uranus and they had some pretty weird children, I can tell you. The one-eyed giant Cyclops caused big Trouble . . . so Uranus created the Underworld for them. A nasty, gloomy place. If you fell from Earth to the Underworld it would take you nine days to land in that place.

But Mother Earth was a strange being. She told her son Cronos to rebel against his father Uranus! Cruel Cronos attacked him and took over the world.

Cronos, he married his sister, Rhea, and they had lots of children but the last one was the greatest . . . me, Zeus. Cronos had thrown his dad off the throne so he couldn't really complain when I threw *him* out. The war lasted ten years but I won in the end. I zapped dad with a thunderbolt.

I shared the top jobs with the rest of the family. I gave the sea to Poseidon and the Underworld to brother Hades. I kept the Earth for myself though I wouldn't want to live down among you dirty little humans. I live on Mount Olympus.

Have your dull brains got the picture? I'll just spell it out once more..."

8 Olympus – home of the gods. Humans can only come here if they're invited, so generally, you smelly little people don't get in!

1 Earth You know what that's like because you live on it.

3 The Underworld a) The River Styx. This is the boundary between the Earth and the Underworld.

6 The Underworld d) Elysian Fields. The goodies go here. A lovely place ... though not as nice as Mount Olympus! From here you can sometimes go back to Earth and live another life or two.

4 The Underworld b) Asphodel Fields. Most humans wander round the Asphodel Fields as ghosts.

10 The Sun Sits in a golden chariot driven by Uncle Helios. Helios once let his son Phaeton drive it. The horses went mad and nearly crashed the sun into the Earth. I killed Phaeton and put my son Apollo in charge.

The sky Held up by Atlas. This is just as well, otherwise it would all fall down and crush you.

9 The Ocean This is a stretch of water that surrounds the earth. Brother Poseidon lives here and controls the wind and waves. He's still not as important as me though!

7 The Underworld e) Islands of the Blessed. If you're so good that you return to the Elysian Fields three times then you are allowed to go come here. You never leave – it's so wonderful you wouldn't want to!

5 The Underworld c) Tartarus. Really evil humans end up in Tartarus. There are some delightful tortures carried out there.

89

"And here I am, Zeus. Chief god. I married my sister, Hera. We happen to have ten top gods to help us. Since you are simple-minded humans and likely to forget them, here they are.

Why am I so good to you?"

The top 10 gods

1 Hephaestus
god of fire and metalwork, an ugly blacksmith, lives in a volcano where he makes gods their armour and jewellery

2 Athena
goddess of arts, Greek cities, spinning, birds and sometimes of war – turned Arachne into a spider

3 Apollo
god of the Sun, young
men, cattle, light, truth,
healing. Lyre-player,
athlete and archer

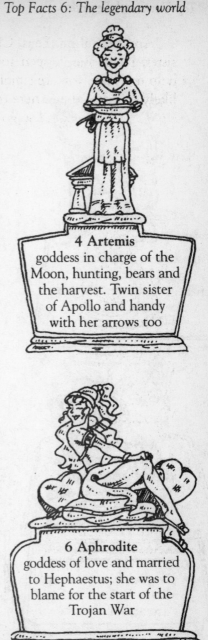

4 Artemis
goddess in charge of the
Moon, hunting, bears and
the harvest. Twin sister
of Apollo and handy
with her arrows too

5 Ares
god of war and unpopular
with gods and with
humans; he goes into
battle with Deimos, the
god of fear

6 Aphrodite
goddess of love and married
to Hephaestus; she was to
blame for the start of the
Trojan War

8 Hermes
messenger to the gods with wings on his hat, wings and snakes on his wand; he leads dead humans to the Underworld

7 Hestia
goddess of the home; she always turns up when there's a sacrifice at an altar and is prayed to before and after meals

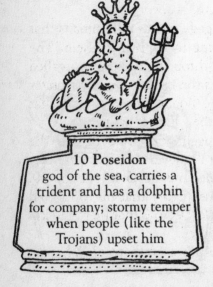

10 Poseidon
god of the sea, carries a trident and has a dolphin for company; stormy temper when people (like the Trojans) upset him

9 Demeter
goddess of crops in summer when she's happy, but she causes winter when her daughter goes to Hades

Legend 5: Oedipus

In Greek legends it seems the only happy people are dead people. In that case there were a lot of happy people in Thebes City. Corpses all over the place.

The gods watched the humans killing and dying and did very little about it. Sometimes they even seemed to enjoy it. They put the humans in impossible positions and watched them struggle to escape.

A favourite trick of the gods was to tell humans that something horrible was going to happen to them. The gods spoke to humans through messengers called "oracles". They told humans the future – usually a pretty nasty future. The more the humans tried to *stop* that thing happening the more they *made* it happen.

Humans are like flies struggling in a spider's web; the more they struggle the more tangled they get. The best example is probably Oedipus, number 5 in our top 10. First the oracle told Oedipus's father that his son would kill him. Then the oracle told Oedipus that he would kill his father and marry his mother.

Did these dreadful horoscopes come true? What do

you think?

If there had been a police force in ancient Thebes then they'd have had the job of trying to untangle the human flies from the sticky webs of the gods . . .

The killer king

Police Headquarters
Thebes
14 June

Report into death of Queen Jocasta (and a few others)
by Detective Inspector Clewless

I was called to the royal Palace of Thebes at 1500 hours on 13 June.

I was shown into the queen's bedroom where her Majesty, Queen Jocasta, was laid on the bed. She was wearing a red dress and a belt of the same material was round her neck. It was very tight, her face was purple and her tongue was sticking out. I loosened the offending belt and asked if her majesty was feeling well. She did not reply, from which I deduced she was *not* well. I am awaiting a doctor's report but I believe she may be dead and suspect that the belt around the neck may have had something to do with this.

I questioned her handmaiden who had called me. "Do you know anything about this?" I asked her.

"She hanged herself," the maid said.

"Hah! A likely story!" I scoffed. "Lay down on the bed and strangled herself with the belt, did she?"

"No!" the maid shouted (and added some words which suggested that my mental ability is not up to the standard of a one-year-old goat). "I found her hanging from the roof beam when I came in with her afternoon wine. I cut her down and called the king. He put her on the bed."

"Hah!" I exclaimed looking into the empty silver goblet on the bedside table. "So, where is the wine?"

"I needed a drink," the handmaiden confessed. "Gave me a bit of a turn, seeing Jocasta strung up like that."

"I arrest you for the theft of the royal wine and for the murder of Queen Jocasta," I said. "I must ask you to accompany me to the Thebes Central Department of Justice Offices."

Again she repeated that she was innocent and that my brain was suffering from a weakness brought on by too much alcohol. I decided it would be wise to hear this woman's story before proceeding to take her in for questioning.

"Why would Queen Jocasta hang herself?" I asked. "She had everything. A nice family, fine young husband in King Oedipus, a fancy palace here and some delicious wine."

"Shall we have a goblet of the wine while I tell you the story?" the handmaiden asked and held up a large jug. I accepted because I believed it may relax her.

"What is your name?" I asked.

"Harmonia," she said.

"Well, Harmonia, what happened to upset Queen Jocasta?" I asked.

"She discovered that King Oedipus, her husband, is really her son!" she said.

"So he married his mother?" I asked.

"That's right."

"And so he became his own stepfather," I reckoned. "Against the law that is. I may have to arrest him. How did this sorry state of affairs come about?" I asked Harmonia.

"It seems that Jocasta and her first husband, Laios, spoke to an oracle and the oracle said their son would kill his father! Then they had a child – Oedipus."

KILL HIS OWN FATHER?!! KIDS! — THEY'RE NOTHIN' BUT TROUBLE!!

"Always a mistake to consult an oracle," I said. And who has to sort the mess out? Us! The Theban Police! If I had my way I'd ban oracles. Ban them!"

"Do you want to hear the story or not?" Harmonia asked.

"Proceed, madam," I said.

"When Laios heard the oracle he put a nail through baby Oedipus's ankles, tied his feet together and left him on a mountainside for the animals to eat him."

"That's attempted murder that is!" I said. "If Laios was alive I'd have to arrest him."

"But he isn't," Harmonia said. "A shepherd saved baby Oedipus and handed him over to King Polybus of Corinth. Oedipus grew up thinking he was the son of Polybus."

NO WONDER HE DEVELOPED A COMPLEX!

"An easy mistake to make."

"But he didn't look like Polybus," Harmonia pointed out. "People remarked on the fact. So Oedipus decided to consult an oracle."

"Oh *no!*" I cried. "Will these royals never learn?"

"Anyway, the oracle refused to speak to him. Said he was going to murder his father . . ."

"Same as King Laios's oracle said," I nodded.

"It also said he'd marry his mother," Harmonia went on.

"Obviously the answer was for Oedipus not to murder anyone or marry anyone," I sniffed. "Obvious when you think about it."

"Of course, *Oedipus* thought King Polybus of Corinth was his father. He decided to leave Corinth and never see King Polybus or Queen Periboa ever again."

"Aha! I can see where the lad came unstuck. A case of mistaken identity. Happens all the time."

Harmonia was tapping her little foot. I could see she was an impatient little madam. Comes of working with the royals, I suppose.

"Do you want to hear what happened?"

"Carry on, miss," I said.

"You may remember when old King Laios kidnapped a boy and made him a slave in the palace? It caused a scandal in the city twenty odd years ago. The boy killed himself."

"I investigated the case myself when I was a young constable. Very sad," I said.

"It brought the curse of the Sphinx on Thebes. You remember the Sphinx, I suppose?" she asked.

"Lor! Yes! Horrible thing. Head of a woman, body of a lion, wings of an eagle and tail of a serpent.

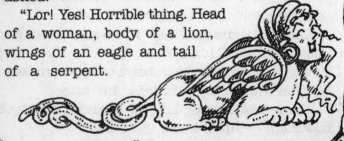

Asked people a riddle. If they couldn't answer then it tore them to pieces and ate them. Of course, we sent officers to arrest the monster. It ate them!"

"That's right. So King Laios went to consult an oracle to see what could be done about the Sphinx," she said.

I shook my head. "Not *another* oracle!" I groaned. "Why can't they just read their horoscopes in the papers? What did *this* oracle tell him?"

"Nothing!" Harmonia said. "He never got there. He was killed on the way. Laios met a young man on a narrow road and told him to get out of the way. The young man refused and killed Laios's chariot driver with his spear."

"That's murder that is," I said. "Shocking lot of murders happen on the roads."

"But that wasn't an end of it!" Harmonia cried. "The young man dragged Laios from the chariot, tangled him in the harness of the chariot and sent the horses racing off. Dragged him to his death!"

"Messy!" I said. "Wonder who this young man was?"

Harmonia drained her wine and filled her goblet again. "Think about it. The oracle told Laios he'd be killed by his son. Oedipus was his son."

"Er . . . let me see . . . you mean? You mean our King Oedipus killed old Laios?"

"Give that cop a coconut," Harmonia said a little rudely. "Oedipus killed his father, Laios."

"Have to have a word with him about that," I said making a note in my book. A kidnapping, an attempted murder, two suicides and two murders. It was a busy day and I'd only been in the palace half an hour.

Harmonia went on, "Then Oedipus set off for the city and met the Sphinx, of course."

"Of course."

"Well, the Sphinx asked him the riddle. 'What has just one name, has four legs in the morning, two in the afternoon and three in the evening. It is weakest when it has the most?'" Harmonia grinned at me and filled my wine goblet. "You're a detective. Solve that little mystery."

CONFUSED??! HOW DO YOU THINK HE FELT?!!!

I drank my wine very slowly and thought about it. "Four legs – two legs – three legs. Dunno what it is but I'd probably arrest it for growing legs without permission."

"You don't know, do you?" the handmaiden smirked. "Go on. Admit it. You don't know."

"I could probably work it out but . . . but . . .

but I am here to investigate the death of Queen Jocasta!" I said.

Harmonia made a very rude noise with her lips. I think the wine was disturbing her brain. "Well, inspector, the answer is a Human Being! As a baby it crawls on four legs, as an adult it walks on two legs and as an old person it walks with a stick."

I sniffed. "Yeah, I knew that. Thought it was the obvious answer. *Too* obvious. Anyway, I guess Oedipus got the right answer."

"He *did*. The Sphinx was so upset she threw herself off a cliff and smashed herself into the ground. Bits of fur and feather all over the place!" she giggled.

I made a note of it. "That makes *three* suicides."

"Oedipus came into Thebes city and he was a hero! The people had heard their king was dead so they offered the crown to Oedipus. He accepted. They also said it would be a good idea for him to marry old Laios's queen, Jocasta!"

OH! THEY MADE A LOVELY COUPLE! HER AND HER TOYBOY!!! EVEN LOOKED ALIKE, THEY DID!!!

"His mother!" I moaned. "The oracle turned out true!"

"It did. They always do," Harmonia said and tapped the side of her nose wisely. It wasn't a very large nose and she missed. That wine was very strong.

"But that happened twenty years ago. Why has Jocasta suddenly decided to kill herself now?"

"The plague, you see," Harmonia whispered.

"Ah, the plague." We've suffered a terrible plague for the last year. Crops dying, people starving, and the gods refusing to do a thing. "I suppose Oedipus sent for another oracle to ask what he could do about the plague?"

"He did!"

"I thought so," I sighed.

"This oracle said the plague would only go when the killer of Laios was brought to justice. So Oedipus sent for the wise man Teiresias. And Teiresias told Oedipus the whole story. How Oedipus had killed Laios, his father, and married Jocasta his mother."

"That would upset Oedipus a bit," I gasped.

"A bit! A BIT!" she wailed. "He's gone next door and he's crying his eyes out! And Jocasta wasn't too happy either." The handmaiden nodded towards the corpse on the bed. "As you can see."

I stood up. The room seemed a bit wobbly and the floor shaky. I took a long drink of wine to steady myself but it didn't seem to do much good. I stumbled and fell on the bed. "Ooops! Sorry, Your Majesty," I said to Queen Jocasta.

She didn't reply. Well, she wouldn't, would she. Not if, as I suspect, she is in fact dead. I looked at her royal face and her royal dress and that's when I noticed a brooch on her left shoulder and a tear on the right shoulder. Something was missing. "Something is missing!" I said.

"What?" the handmaiden said.

"There should be another brooch on this shoulder to match that one!" I told her.

"Brilliant" Harmonia said. "You should be a detective!"

"I should," I agreed. Then I thought about it. "Er, actually, I am a detective!"

"Then do some detecting," Harmonia sneered. "Where do you think the brooch is? Eh?"

"Who found the body?"

"I did."

"What did you do when you found the body?"

"Told Oedipus then sent for you."

"So . . . the brooch was taken by you, Harmonia!"

"Or by you, inspector!"

"Ah . . . good thinking. Yes, I could be the thief," I nodded.

"So where have you put the brooch?" she asked.

"I've forgotten!"

"Hey! Maybe you didn't steal it after all!" she said.

"Well, if *you* didn't steal it and *I* didn't steal it then who *did*?" I said and my brain hurt with thinking about it.

"It must have been King Oedipus!" she cried.

"Pah!" I snorted. "What would he want with a brooch? He must have hundreds of them?"

"Why not go and ask him?" she said. "He's just next door."

"Crying his eyes out?"

"Crying his eyes out!" she smirked.

I pushed myself off the bed and walked to the large bronze doors into the king's room. I rapped hard on the door. It didn't make a sound but it hurt my hand a lot. I turned the handle and walked into the room. "Oedipus, sir?" I said.

It was gloomy in there. He'd closed the shutters. Then I heard a moaning. He was lying on the bed, his fists clutched to his eyes. "I married my mum!" he wailed.

"Never mind, sir. I'm sure we can sort it all out. If you'd just like to come down to the station, and make a statement."

"I can't!" he screamed. "I'd never find it."

"It's in the middle of the city. Plain as the nose on your face," I said.

"I can't *see* the nose on my face," he moaned and slid his hands down. What a mess. "I've clawed my eyes out with the pin on Jocasta's brooch. It's my way of punishing myself!"

I backed out of the door feeling just a little sick. "When the doc comes to look at Jocasta he'll have a look at those wounds for you," I promised and closed the door behind me.

"Well?" Harmonia asked.

"Well," I said, consulting my notebook. "That's one kidnapping, one case of marrying your own mother, two murders and three suicides. An average sort of day in the life of a legend, I'd say. The good news is I've solved the mystery of the missing brooch." I snapped my notebook shut. "Case closed, I think."

"What am I going to do?" Harmonia snivelled.

"Do?" I smiled. "If I were you I'd go and get a bucket and mop. You're going to need it next door. Cheerio. Nice meeting you miss."

I departed from the Royal Palace at 1600 hours.

Top Facts 5: Gory gods

The Sphinx ate people. It ate travellers on the road to Thebes. This was the gods' way of punishing Laios for kidnapping a boy.

You may think this is a bit unfair. Imagine being one of those travellers on the road to Thebes. The Sphinx stops you and asks you the riddle. You get it wrong ... the Sphinx wraps her serpent's tail around your neck and begins to strangle you.

"Aaaacccch!" you splutter. "What have I done to deserve this?"

"This is the gods' way of punishing Laios!" the Sphinx explains as it chokes the last drop of air out of you.

"So why don't you strangle Laios?" you gasp. These are the last words you ever say. The last words you ever hear are the Sphinx's as she mutters, "Good question that. Jolly good question!"

The gods, the heroes and the villains of Greek legend came up with a lot of different ways of torturing or killing their victims. Here's a truly terrible top ten ...

Messy murder and mutilation

1 Dionysus invented wine. Women formed groups of supporters to drink his wine. It turned them wild and they ran around the mountains having picnics, drinking wine and eating wild animals that they tore apart and ate raw. Pentheus, King of Thebes, did not like this idea so Dionysus visited him and made him

drunk . . . and got revenge. Drunken Pentheus said he'd like to see these wild women on a picnic, so Dionysus placed him on the top of a tall pine tree so he'd have a good view – and nowhere to escape! The women pulled down the tree and tore Pentheus apart. Pentheus's mother, one of the drinkers, took the head back to Thebes and drunkenly claimed it was the head of a lion. When she discovered the sober truth she went off her head with grief – but not as off her head as Pentheus.

2 A crew of Greek heroes were with their captain Odysseus, travelling home from the Trojan Wars. Odysseus was a bit careless in straying into the giant Cyclops Polyphemus's cave. He made things worse by telling the giant what a great fighter he, Odysseus, was. The heroes seem to have caught Polyphemus on a lunch break and he swallowed them without even stopping to put tomato ketchup on. He put the rest in the cupboard for later and had a snack of another four before Odysseus rescued his men.

3 The god Pan was an ugly creature

with the face and body of a man but the legs, feet and horns of a goat. Would you like to marry him? The nymph Syrinx didn't. As he chased her she hid in shallow water at the edge of a river. When Pan arrived she begged her sisters to disguise her – they turned her into a clump of reeds. Pan grabbed the reeds and cut them up into a set of pipes so he could play on her whenever he wanted. They are now known as Pan pipes and the mournful sound they make could well be the pathetic voice of poor Syrinx.

4 Zeus and Prometheus had fought on the same side in the wars against the old gods, the Titans. Zeus asked Prometheus to create the human race which he did. But Zeus told Prometheus that humans were not allowed to have fire. When Prometheus disobeyed he suffered the torture of having his liver torn out by an eagle. But the worst part was that the liver grew back every night and the eagle returned every day to tear it out again. Prometheus was finally rescued by the great hero-god Heracles. Heracles strangled the poor eagle ... who was only doing his job!

108

5 The hero Theseus met the giant Sinis on his travels. Sinis would meet a traveller and ask the traveller to grab hold of a bent pine tree. As the traveller grabbed the tree, Sinis would let go suddenly, the traveller would fly into the air and be crushed as he landed. Sinis then bent two trees together and tied the victim between them. When he let go the trees would tear the traveller apart. Sinis seems to have done this for fun! Theseus was too quick – he let go of the tree first, Sinis flew in the air and crashed to Earth. It was Sinis who was torn apart by the two pine trees. "Serves him right," Theseus said.

6 Theseus was invited to stay in the giant Prokrustes's magic bed. Prokrustes said it fitted everyone who slept in it. The truth is Prokrustes made *them* fit the *bed*. If the victim was too short then Prokrustes stretched them and tore their limbs out till they fitted. If the visitor was too tall then Prokrustes cut bits off to make them shorter. Crafty Theseus knew what to expect and trapped the giant. He reckoned Prokrustes was too tall and used the giant's axe to hack bits off and make him suffer the way the other travellers had suffered. As the old proverb says, "You have made your bed and now you must lie in it."

7 Antigone was in a tricky position. Her brother had been killed in a battle with Kreon. The cruel King of Thebes said the dead body of Antigone's brother had to stay on the battlefield and be eaten by wild animals. But the laws of the gods say a relative must bury a dead relative. Antigone threw soil over her brother's battered body and was arrested. Kreon had her walled up in a tomb. Kreon was warned by a fortune-teller that he must set her free – or else. He went to open the tomb but found she had hanged herself. Kreon's wife then killed herself so he suffered the loss of a loved one just as Antigone had.

8 Medea was a mean woman. Beautiful Glaucis wanted to marry Jason . . . but so did Medea. Medea gave Glaucis a magical crown and dress to wear. They burst into flames and killed her on the eve of the wedding. The wedding was off and Jason was a miserable hero.

SOMETHING OLD?

Barbecuing Glaucis was just one of many nasty tricks by Medea. When a king opposed her she persuaded the king's daughters to boil him alive, which they did!

9 The ancient Titans tore the newly-born Dionysus into pieces and boiled the pieces in a pot because Hera, Zeus's wife persuaded them to. But don't worry too much about the boiled baby. His grandmother, the goddess Rhea, collected all the pieces and joined him back together again. He was as good as new . . . which is better than being as good as stew.

10 Athene did not like human men to see her bathing . . . yet she seemed to make a habit of being caught in the act! She blinded a hunter, Tiresias, when she caught him peeking.

Match the murder

You've just read the top 10 murder stories. But, as your teacher would say, "Have you been paying attention? Eh?" Test yourself with this murderously maddening quiz. Anything less than a top 10 out of 10 mark and you can give yourself a detention.

Match the right killer with the right victim and the right reason.

THE KILLER	THE VICTIM	THE REASON
1 The god Dionysus	A bent two pine trees together, tied one arm and leg of Sinis to one tree, the other arm and leg to the other tree. Then he let the trees spring apart	I because the victim was a cruel killer.
2 The king of Thebes, Kreon	B ate two Greek sailors	II because the victim had disobeyed an order and given human beings the gift of fire.
3 The hero Theseus	C had young Antigone walled up in a tomb alive and left to die	III because the victim didn't believe in the power of the god.
4 The hero Theseus also	D blinded the hunter Tiresias	IV because the victim refused to marry the killer.
5 The goat-god Pan	E tore the newly-born Dionysus into pieces and boiled the pieces in a pot	V because the victims dared to ask the killer for food.

VI because the killer was jealous and wanted to marry the victim's lover.

VII because this was the victim's own favourite way of killing off travellers.

VIII because they were persuaded by jealous Hera.

IX because the victim saw the killer with no clothes on, bathing in a stream.

X because the victim tried to bury her dead brother.

F had king Pentheus of Thebes torn apart by drunken women

G gave beautiful Glaucis a crown and a dress to wear. They burst into flames and killed her

H turned the nymph Syrinx into a set of musical pipes

I had the god Prometheus chained to a rock where an eagle swooped down to tear out his liver

J placed the giant Prokrustes on a bed and used the giant's own axe to cut off his feet and head till he fitted the bed

6 The goddess of hunting, Artemis

7 The giant Cyclops, Polyphemus

8 The god Zeus

9 The giant old gods, the Titans

10 The witch Medea

Answers

1 F III, 2 C X, 3 A VII, 4 J I, 5 H IV, 6 D IX, 7 B V, 8 I II, 9 E VIII, 10 G VI

Legend 4: The Labours of Heracles*

Some heroes have a really tough life. Poor Heracles had problems from the day he was born. The goddess Hera did not like him and decided to kill him. So she sent two huge serpents to destroy him when he was still a baby. You would expect a couple of serpents to wrap themselves around baby Heracles, crush him and maybe swallow him, wouldn't you? Hera expected that – and so did the serpents, probably.

Imagine the shock they must have got when Heracles wrapped a baby hand around each serpent neck and choked them to death!

As a schoolboy he beat his music teacher over the head with a lyre and killed him. Hercules was put on trial for murder but set free when he said the music teacher was bullying him. (You must *never* try hitting *your* music teacher over the head with a piano. You could well damage the piano.)

Then, when he was a young man he met a hungry lion.

* You might have heard of Hercules? That's just the Roman way of saying Heracles. Heracles is his proper, Greek, name!

Again you'd expect it to tear him to pieces and eat him, bones and all. But, no. He killed the lion with his bare hands, wore the skin of the lion as a cloak and its head as a helmet. (Hopefully he scooped the brains out first.) Hera must have been *really* fed up with Heracles by now – and the lion can't have been too happy either.

So the goddess came up with a sneaky trick. She sent a fit of madness into his brain and he killed his wife and three children. He was so upset he wanted to kill himself. He was good at killing by now and he'd have made a good job of it. But the Oracle at Delphi sent him a message from the gods. It told him to become the servant of King Eurystheus and do whatever he was told.

Eurystheus could have made Heracles wash the dishes, walk the dogs or babysit the children. But the king was pretty mean. He gave Heracles twelve terrible tasks to perform. *Impossible* tasks in fact. But a hero can do the impossible.

School teachers are a bit like King Eurystheus and enjoy setting impossible tasks. If Eurystheus had been a teacher he'd have set out the tasks on a work-sheet and expected Heracles to report back on each one . . . Naturally Eurystheus wanted Heracles to fail in all of the tasks so some of his marking may have been very unfair!

Here are Heracles' work-sheets for the top 10 tasks he had to perform . . .

The Standard Attainment Tests (SATs) of Heracles

Standard Attainment Test for Heracles 1
Task: Kill the lion of Nemea. This lion is extremely large and is a real nuisance. Problem 1: Find the lion. Since it's eaten everyone in the area there is no one to tell you where it lives! Problem 2: The lion cannot be harmed by any weapon of iron, bronze or stone.

Student report: I wandered round for a few days till I spotted the lion returning to its cave. My arrows bounced off its skin, my sword bent on its back and my club shattered on its head. So I waited for it to come out next day and wrestled with it. Finally I choked it with my hands even though it bit off one of my fingers. My knife wouldn't cut it so I used one of the lion's claws to skin it. I use its weapon-proof skin as armour and head as a helmet. I threw away my old lion-skin cloak. (Well, it was getting a bit smelly anyway.)

<u>Teacher Comment & Mark</u>: Very poor. Level 3. Your hands are weapons so using your hands to kill the lion was cheating. Must do better.

Standard Attainment Test for Heracles 2

Task: Kill the Hydra. Problem 1: Find it somewhere in the deadly sucking swamp at Lerna. Problem 2: The Hydra has a huge dog body, nine snake heads (one of which cannot be killed) and it is so venomous even its breath or its footprint can kill a human.

Student report: As I crossed the swamp a huge crab nipped at my foot. This upset me so I killed it and set about chopping off Hydra heads. But every time I cut off a head there were three more grew in its place. I cut off three heads and then there were nine so I stopped cutting because I'd run out of fingers to count on. I then called to my nephew Iolaus for help. He burned the stump of each neck as I chopped off the head. This stopped new heads growing. The head that couldn't be killed was buried. Sadly, I lost a toe in the battle. Now I can only count up to 18.

Teacher Comment & Mark: Very poor. Level 2. Using your nephew to help is cheating. Must try harder.

Standard Attainment Test for Heracles 3
Task: Capture the stag of Artemis. Problem 1: The stag (with golden antlers and hooves of brass) is so shy it runs away from humans and can never be caught. Problem 2: The stag is too fast for any human to catch. (Especially a big, lumbering brute of a human hero.)

Student report: First I tired the stag out by chasing it as far as Istria. After a year of running I cornered it. Then I fired an arrow that pinned its legs together. I threw it over my shoulder and returned with the animal. Artemis was a bit upset because she's a goddess and I'd pinched her stag. But I showed her it wasn't really hurt and promised to release it after Eurystheus had seen it and she forgave me.

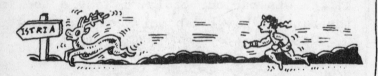

Teacher Comment & Mark:

Below average. Level 4. No time limit was set for this task but a whole year is a ridiculous time to take. Must work faster.

Standard Attainment Test for Heracles 4
Task: Clean out the Augean stables. Problem 1: King Augeius has the filthiest cattle yard in the world. It has never been cleared out in 30 years and the cattle dung is metres deep. Problem 2: A time limit is set for this task. The student has just 24 hours or one day . . . whichever is the shorter . . . and must not have any help.

Student report: I agreed with the king that I'd take one in every ten cattle if I cleaned out his yard. First I made a hole in the wall of the cattle yard at one end and a hole at the far end. Then I built a dam across two rivers till they overflowed and swept through the king's stables instead. The stables were washed perfectly clean and the poisonous smell has gone from the land.

RIVER WATER.

Teacher Comment & Mark :

*Working towards Level 1.
(In other words "failed".) The
river gods cleaned the yard, not
the student. And agreeing to work
for payment is not allowed. Must
read test paper more carefully.*

Standard Attainment Test for Heracles 5
Task: Drive off the man-eating birds of Lake Stymphalus. Problem 1: These birds have bronze claws, beaks and wings. Their poisonous droppings have poisoned the crops of the land around. They can fire their feathers like arrows and they kill and eat humans. Problem 2: The swampy lake is too wet to walk on and too thick with mud to sail a boat on. No one can get to the birds.

Student report: The goddess Athene gave me a pair of bronze castanets. I stood on the shore of the lake and clattered the castanets. The birds were so frightened they rose into the air in terror. The ones that flew over me were shot down with my arrows. The others escaped to the Isle of Ares and are too scared ever to return.

Teacher Comment & Mark: Not satisfactory. Level 3. The birds have been driven off but may return some day. Must be more thorough.

Standard Attainment Test for Heracles 6
Task: Bring the mad bull of Crete to King Eurystheus.
Problem 1: This powerful creature is destroying the crops.
When farmers build walls it just knocks them down.
Problem 2: It bellows out scorching flames that can melt
a man's armour and cook him inside.

Student report: The king of Crete offered
to help me but I told him this was a SAT
that I had to do for myself. I sneaked up
behind the creature so it couldn't roast me
with its breath. As I wrestled with the
bull I wrapped an arm around its nose so
it couldn't open its mouth and breathe out
fire. I then dragged it to King Eurystheus
but the king refused to see me personally.

Teacher Comment & Mark: Fairly
good. Level 5. But not a very
difficult task. Anyone can wrestle
with a bull. And, after all, it was
allowed to escape afterwards and
is now terrorising another place.
More care needed.

Standard Attainment Test for Heracles 7
Task: Bring back the man-eating mares of King Diomedes. Problem 1: These four mares are tethered with iron chains in bronze stables and guarded by the king's most bloodthirsty soldiers. Problem 2: King Diomedes feeds them on the flesh of human guests.

Student report: I killed the guards by creeping up behind them and breaking their necks. This is quieter and not as messy as chopping them with swords. Then I drove the mares down to the sea where they were guarded by my friend Abderus. (Sadly, when I returned, I found they had eaten Abderus.) I went to collect the evil King Diomedes, I bashed him on the head with my club and threw him to his horses. They enjoyed this fresh meat - in fact it was extremely fresh because he was still alive as they ate him - and they were so full of food they followed me tamely back.

Teacher Comment & Mark: Average.
Killing the king was not part of the
S.A.T. Losing Abderus was extremely
careless - servants cost money. Must
think harder about these tasks.

Standard Attainment Test for Heracles 8
Task: Get the belt of Queen Hippolyta. Problem 1:
Hipollyta is Queen of the Amazon Women and she wears
the belt all the time – even in bed. Problem 2: the
Amazon women are the fiercest fighters on Earth. Even a
super hero could not defeat them all by himself.

Student report: I took an army of the best
Greek soldiers (just to be on the safe
side) and visited Queen Hippolyta. She was
a really charming lady. I simply asked her
for the belt and she offered to let me take
it. Unfortunately, the goddess Hera had
been spreading the word that I was planning
to kidnap Hippolyta. The Amazon women
attacked my army. I thought Hippolyta had
given the order to attack so I killed her.
Several hundred Greek soldiers and Amazon
warriors died as well as the queen. But at
least I got the belt.

QUEEN
HIPPOLYTA

Teacher Comment & Mark: Below
average. Level 2. A very messy piece
of work. Blood all over the place just
to get a belt. Must try to work
more neatly in future – or learn to
clean up after himself.

Standard Attainment Test for Heracles 9
Task: Fetch a golden apple of the Hesperides. These apples are eaten by the gods on Olympus and they keep them young. Problem 1: They are guarded by nymphs called the Hesperides and no one knows just where their orchard is. Problem 2: The Hesperides are the daughters of the great god Atlas who holds up the sky on his shoulders. He may not be pleased if someone steals his daughters' apples.

Student report: I went and asked Atlas where the apples were growing. The old god said he would fetch me some apples if I would hold the sky while he went to get them. Unfortunately, when he returned with the apples, he didn't want to take the sky off my shoulders - he'd enjoyed his little trip to the garden of the Hesperides! I agreed to keep it a little while longer but asked him to hold it while I settled it more comfortably on my shoulders. As he took the weight I grabbed the apples and ran off. Atlas is stuck with the boring job once more.

Teacher Comment & Mark: Below standard. Level 1 Getting someone else to do the task is almost cheating. Marks deducted for telling lies to a god.

Standard Attainment Test for Heracles 10
Task: Bring back the three-headed dog Cerberus from the gates of Hades. Problem 1: It's a long way to the Underworld where Cerberus guards the gates. Problem 2: Cerberus is a vicious, three-headed animal that has never been tamed.

Student report: The goddess Athene showed me the way to the Underworld where I met the god Hades and his wife Persephone. I released a few dead friends from their tortures in the Underworld then asked Hades if I could borrow his watch dog. Hades agreed but only if I could take him without using my club or my arrows. Now Cerberus has three heads but they all join on to just one throat. I grabbed that throat and held it till the dog obeyed me. His stinging tail tried to lash me but my lion-skin cloak protected me. I had to half drag and half carry the beast but I did reach the court of Eurystheus in the end. Since this was my last task I took great pleasure in killing three of the King Eurystheus's sons. And, if King Eurystheus doesn't agree that I have passed my tests, I may have to kill him too . . .

Teacher Comment & Mark:
Pass. Level 10! Well done!

Top Facts 4: Hooray Heroes

Heracles was certainly the greatest hero of Greek legend. He never stopped fighting, killing, rescuing and protecting. Unfortunately, a lot of people got hurt when Heracles did his heroics. He took part in a sporting boxing match. First he knocked out the champion's teeth, then he broke his skull and killed him . . . then he said, "Sorry!"

But Heracles wasn't the only hero around in Greek legend. If you'd been a woman going to a computer dating agency then there'd have been lots of heroes for you to choose from.

Super men

1 Name: Ganymede

Family: Son of King Tros of Troy

Career: Far too good looking to stay on Earth. Zeus sent an eagle to pick him up and carry him to Olympus where he is cup-bearer to the gods.

"I'm Ganymede...You'll be starry-eyed over me!"

Features: Can be seen in the sky every night when he becomes the star cluster known as Aquarius. Enjoys keeping fit, good wine and astronomy. Dislikes bird watching.

2 Name: Cadmus

Family: Son of the king of Phoenicia

Career: Founded the city of Thebes; killed a dragon, sowed its teeth as seeds which sprouted into armed men. The armed men attacked him

"I'm Cadmus............ 'Letters' meet up soon!"

but he turned them against each other till only five survived. Cadmus and the five became leaders of the new city of Thebes. He is supposed to have invented the Greek alphabet.

Features: Brave and reliable leader. Likes adventure, killing dragons and reading. Dislikes gardening.

3 Name: Pelops

Family: Son of Tantalus

Career: Killed by his father and served to the gods at a feast. The gods brought him back to life. Demeter had already eaten his shoulder so she gave him a new

"I'm Pelops............ They say I'm tasty!"

ivory one. He became Olympic chariot champion after bribing his opponent to lose!

Features: Daring and cheeky. Enjoys horseracing, keep fit and vegetarian food. Dislikes stewed meat.

4 Name: Daedalus

Family: Father of Icarus

Career: Great inventor from Athens who designed the Labyrinth on Crete to trap the bull-man Minotaur inside. When he upset King Minos he was put in prison but invented wax and feather wings to fly to freedom. Unfortunately, young Icarus got carried away, flew too near the Sun and his wax wings melted. The crash into the sea killed him.

"I'm Daedalus......
Come, fly with me..!!"

Features: Cunning and very intelligent. Enjoys working with his hands, foreign travel and hang gliding. Dislikes sunbathing.

5 Name: Arion

Family: Son of Cycleus

Career: Brilliant musician. In one contest he won all of the top prizes and set off to sail home with them. The sailors decided to throw him overboard and steal his valuable prizes. Luckily his singing in the water attracted dolphins who saved him.

"I'm Arion.......Let's
make music together"

Features: Cheerful and lucky. Enjoys reading poetry, making music and trips to marine parks. Dislikes sea cruises.

6 Name: Calchas

Family: Son of Thestors, a Trojan

Career: Priest of the god Apollo with the gift of being able to see into the future. Usually his forecasts are very gloomy and make him very unpopular but he goes ahead and gives them anyway. He told Greek king Agamemnon to sacrifice his daughter and Agamemnon did. It was Calchas's idea to build a wooden horse to defeat the Trojans.

"I'm Calchas ... I see a future for us!!"

Features: Serious and determined. Likes collecting crystal balls, carving wooden horses and making sacrifices to Apollo. Dislikes being asked to name the winners of next week's horse races.

7 Name: Diomedes

Family: Son of Tydeus and Deipyle

Career: Fought for Greece in the Trojan War. Very brave and willing to fight anyone. He even had the cheek to wound the goddess Aphrodite and drive the god of war Ares from the field because they were helping the enemy.

"I'm Diomedes .... You're not Trojan, are you?"

Features: Brave and even stupidly brave. Likes killing Trojans, killing human friends of Trojans and wounding gods who are friends of Trojans. Dislikes Trojans.

8 Name: Asclepius
Family: Son of god Apollo and human Coronis
Career: Brilliant doctor who invented many wonderful cures for human illnesses, pains and suffering. When he actually brought a human patient back to life the god Zeus was furious and killed him. But Zeus forgave Asclepius and brought him back to life again.

"I'm Asclepius...you'll have no complaints!"

Features: Caring and clever. Likes visiting hospitals, wearing a white coat and cutting up dead bodies. Dislikes graveyards.

9 Name: Hyacinthus
Family: Son of a Spartan prince
Career: Extremely good looking and sporty. Became a special friend of Apollo, god of the Sun. This made the West Wind very jealous. One day, as Apollo taught Hyacinthus to throw a

"I'm Hyacinthus...Let's 'discus' our future..!!"

discus, the West Wind caught the discus and threw it back into the young human's face. This rearranged his good looks quite a lot. Where his blood fell the first Hyacinth flowers grew.

Features: Fun loving and athletic. Likes walking in the Sun, plastic surgery and the sport called throw-the-boomerang-discus-then-duck. Dislikes flowers but especially hyacinths.

10 Name: Telemachus

Family: Son of Odysseus and Penelope

Career: When his father went off to fight in the Trojan Wars the young Telemachus felt he had to look after his mother, Penelope. Lots of men came to chat up Penelope and Telemachus became very angry, especially when they made fun of him. When Odysseus returned the young Telemachus helped his dad massacre all of these strange men. They hid the strangers, shields and spears first!

"I'm Telemachus....I'm no mummy's boy!!"

Features: Loyal and devoted son. Likes his mum, his dad and his mum (again). Dislikes nasty strange men.

Of all of these Greek legendary heroes, which would *you* choose?

Legend 3: Jason and the Argonauts

If you're going to be a hero then you have to have a "task". Not a simple task. If your mother says, "Pop down to the shop and get us a bottle of milk, love," then you do not become a hero . . . not even if you brave the bullies at number twenty, defeat the roaring Rovers on the road and overcome the Zebra at the crossing.

No. The task has to be dangerous, difficult, deadly and probably impossible. Like when your mother asks you to fetch *three* bottles of milk even though you only have two hands to carry them! Then you need help. You need a whole gang of heroes.

One of the greatest Greek gangs was led by Jason. These heroes sailed in the ship, the *Argo* so they called themselves the Argonauts.

Jason's uncle was looking after the kingdom until Jason was old enough to take over. But when Jason grew up his uncle refused to hand it back . . . unless Jason could get the fleece from a golden ram in Colchis. Of course, Colchis was a long and dangerous journey away and the fleece was guarded by a deadly serpent.

Like many heroes Jason had a lot of help (and a bit of cheating) from a woman called Medea. She was the daughter of King Aeetes of Colchis, the guardian of the Golden Fleece.

Medea fell in love with hero Jason (some unfortunate woman always does in Greek legends), but never had a happy life. Her story is number 3 in our top ten.

If there had been magazines with Agony Aunts then Medea would have written to one of them to ask for help

. . .The magic of Medea

Dear Aunt Angela,

I am writing to you for advice. I am at my wits' end and don't know who else to turn to. The man I love has deserted me for another woman. I want to kill him or even kill this other woman. Sometimes I feel like killing myself, but I know that wouldn't do any good.

I adored Jason from the moment he stepped ashore in our kingdom of Colchis. He had almost fifty heroes with him to help row his boat but it was Jason who caught my eye.

He's was a tall, handsome young man wearing a

close-fitting leather tunic and a leopard skin. His long hair was even more beautiful than mine!

My father, Aeetes, is king of Colchis and he welcomed the heroes – though he was a bit nervous about having all these warriors in our palace, as you can imagine. Jason explained that our Golden Fleece was haunted by a ghost that was cursing his kingdom. If the Golden Fleece returned in his ship, the *Argo*, then the curse on his kingdom would be lifted.

It seems the *Argo* was built of timber from Mount Pelion except for the front piece – the prow, he called it – which was made from oak brought by the goddess Athena herself. The oak prow could talk and foretell the future. That's magic and I understand magic. I understand it very, very well.

I sat at my father's left hand while Jason and his Argonauts told us of the adventures they had had on the way to Colchis. They had lost a man drowned by nymphs – the nymphs fell in love with him and dragged him under the water to their home. They drove off the fearsome Harpies that were plaguing an old prophet and they sailed through the dreadful clashing rocks of the Symplegades. The Argonauts had visited the murderous women of Lemnos, defeated the six-armed giants of Arcton and massacred the noble King Cyzicus and his army – by accident.

I listened to the stories and was enchanted.

I believe the goddess Aphrodite's little son Eros hit my heart with a golden arrow. (As you know, this makes someone fall hopelessly in love.) I also believe the gods had something to do with this. I'd always loved my magic arts more than I ever loved a man – until I met Jason.

Jason and his heroes had battled their way to Colchis and asked for the fleece. It seemed fair enough to me. After all we have no use for the

Golden Fleece ourselves. Father just keeps it in a scared grove, guarded by a fierce serpent. He doesn't even bother looking at it. I would have given the fleece to Jason on condition that he took me for his wife! But father's spiteful. He always liked my younger brother better than me.

First my father threatened to cut out their tongues and lop off their hands. I whispered to my father that this would not look good with the gods. A king cannot kill or injure a guest. So father set Jason some impossible tasks before he would let him take the fleece.

Jason's first task was to take two fire-breathing bulls, harness them and use them to plough the field of Ares. Then Jason had to sow the seeds of serpent's

teeth in the ploughed field. Jason knew the legend. He knew that every tooth would spring up into an armed man and the armed men would attack him.

The young leader of the Argonauts frowned, then he looked at me. I smiled a secret smile that said, "I'll help you." He turned to my father and said, "I agree!"

Father gave a sour grin and said Jason must perform

the tasks the next day. After a feast that night he was to sleep in the palace then win the fleece or die.

Jason drank little, though my father and his guards drank themselves into an early sleep. I followed Jason to his room. In the flickering light of the flaming rushes I said, "You will die if you have no help."

"I know," he said.

"But I have the power to help you. All I ask is that you will marry me and take me back with you," I said.

Jason agreed. "I swear by all the gods of Olympus to keep faith with Medea forever, if she helps me win the Golden Fleece."

I took out a flask from under my robe. It held the blood-red juice of the two-stalked Caucasian Crocus. I told him to bathe his body, his spear and his shield in the juice and he would be protected from the breath of the bulls.

The next day it was still a great struggle to harness the bulls but the hero did it and ploughed the field of Ares. My spiteful father sneered and said he'd wait until my Jason sowed the dragon's teeth. But I had taught my hero how to fight the soldiers who sprang up as soon as each seed hit the ground. He threw a heavy stone among them. The stone hit one who blamed another and they started fighting amongst themselves and killing one another.

Soon there was just one weak and bloodied warrior left and Jason carved him with his sword. He turned to the king, my father and asked, "Now can I take the fleece?"

My father was furious. He said that he would let him take the fleece next day. But as we left the field of Ares I heard him murmur to the captain of the guard, "I want that Jason murdered, and his crew, and I want the *Argo* burned."

I stayed behind and led the Argonauts to the secret, hidden spot where the Golden Fleece was hung. The guarding serpent had a thousand coils and was larger than the heroes' boat. It was born from the blood of the monster Typhon. I took the juice from fresh-cut sprigs of juniper and rubbed this in the dragon's eyelids. All the while I muttered an ancient spell. Soon the creature lay asleep and Jason took the Golden Fleece.

Jason hurried to the ship and made the oars and sail ready while I went back to the palace. I went to the room of my young brother Apsyrtus and said, "Would you like to sail with the Argonauts, brother?"

I knew that was his dream. He followed me through secret passageways and crept out of the palace down the path to the harbour. Jason helped us both aboard though he was puzzled when I brought my brother Apsyrtus. "You'll see," I said. "You'll see!"

I knew my father would not let the Golden Fleece leave Colchis without a fight. When we'd been at sea for less than a day, the lookout said he spied a sail. A warship from Colchis was following. It had three hundred oars and it was gaining fast. I could make out the figure of my father in the bow, purple cloak, red face outlined against 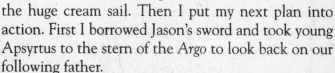 the huge cream sail. Then I put my next plan into action. First I borrowed Jason's sword and took young Apsyrtus to the stern of the *Argo* to look back on our following father.

"Look over the side of the boat," I told him.

The boy leaned forward. "I can't see anything."

"Lean further over," I said.

When half his body was over the side I brought the sword down. With one blow his head leapt off and fell into the sea. My father saw the beheading. I heard his cry. I heard him shout an order. Soon the sail was lowered and the oars stopped. Fishing nets were lowered over the side of the warship to try to catch the head of his dear son.

The body lay bleeding on the deck of the *Argo* and three times I licked up blood and spat it out to stop his ghost from haunting me.

The Argonauts bent their backs and rowed away. But an hour later that great cream sail was catching us again. This time I lopped off a hand from dead Apsyrtus's arm and let it fall into the sea.

League on league I cut my brother into pieces. The warship and my father had to slow each time or else he'd have no whole body for burial. The next day the warship had disappeared and we had sailed clear of the Black Sea.

That night the prow of the ship spoke. It said the *Argo* would sail no further while I was on board. I was a murderess and I would have to walk. Jason took the Golden Fleece and so we set off overland to reach his home.

When we arrived at his kingdom Jason still needed my help. His evil uncle refused to give up the throne. Jason could not kill the old man because the gods punish anyone who kills a member of their family. But I could arrange his uncle's death.

I entered the palace disguised as an old woman. I told the old king and his daughters that I had the secret of youth. I made spells and drank juices, threw off my disguise and appeared to them as myself – a young woman! Then I showed them an old ram. I cut it up, boiled it in a pot and pulled out a frisky lamb that I'd hidden under my cloak. I told them I could do the same for the old king and they believed me.

First I sent him to sleep the way I had the serpent in Colchis. Then I told the daughters to cut him up and boil the pieces. This they did. Imagine their disappointment when he didn't come back to life as a young man!

So the old king was dead and Jason took his throne without having to spill his blood. I had won the Golden Fleece for Jason and lifted the curse from his country; I'd helped him escape and won him back his throne. Of course, he married me and made me his wife.

We could have lived happily forever more. We really could. But Jason has turned against me. He wants a divorce. His only excuse is that I poisoned

the king of Corinth to win another throne. So what if I did? I did it for Jason. Now he wants to marry some young princess of Corinth called Glaucis.

What have I done to deserve this sort of cruelty? All I ever did was try to make my Jason happy. As I said, I am tempted to kill Jason but I do still love him. What would you do dear, Aunt Angela? Please advise me.

Dear Medea,
Men can be terribly ungrateful. Heroes are the worst of all. You are clearly a caring and loving wife. There is obviously only one thing you can do. You have to kill young Glaucis. (With a name like that she'll be better off dead.)

Call my hotline to hear my advice on disposing of unwanted love rivals. This month's special will tell you how to make a burning robe. Make the robe, steep it in my special recipe and leave it to dry. When it is dry, offer it as a gift to your enemy. As soon as your enemy puts it on they will feel burning pains shooting through their body and in no time they will be dead. The robe clings to the skin and anyone trying to help your enemy will simply tear their skin off. It's a nasty way to die, but she *is* a husband stealer and deserves it. Plus, you will have another great advantage . . . no one will ever try to steal your husband again!

May I wish you the very best of luck, Medea. You are a girl after my own heart. I'm sure you'll soon put a stop to Jason's chasin'! Good luck!

Aunt Angela

In fact Glaucis burst into flames and killed everyone in the palace except Jason! He was furious and Medea had to flee for her life.

The gods liked Medea's tough spirit so much they gave her a happy home in the afterlife in the Elysian Fields.

But Jason had broken his promise to Medea – he had sworn by "all the gods of Olympus to keep faith." He was overcome with misery and decided to hang himself. He threw a rope over the magical wooden prow of the *Argo*. But the old ship was rotten. The prow snapped off, fell on his head and killed him!

Life can be lousy for a legendary hero.

Top Facts 3: Have you seen this criminal?

The murdering Medea fled to other countries before finally marrying King Aegeus and settling down in Athens. Nowadays she would not have got away so easily. Her picture would have been on the front pages of newspapers. Even a hundred years ago her face would have appeared on wanted posters.

But the Greeks didn't have wanted posters. That's a shame really, because there were some real villains around who deserved to be caught. The top 10 Greek villains are probably the following . . .

WANTED

1 Name: Sisyphus

Wanted for: Treason and unlawful imprisonment. Betrayed the secrets of his best friend Zeus. When he was sent to Hades he tricked the god of the Underworld and left Hades fastened in his own chains. A sly character.

Sentence: If caught he will spend the rest of his time in the Underworld where he will roll a large stone up a steep hill – every time it reaches the top it will roll back down.

Reward: A free trip to Hades for anyone reporting the whereabouts of Sisyphus.

WANTED

2 Name: Ixion

Wanted for: Murder and attempted kidnapping. Although Ixion killed his father-in-law, Zeus was ready to forgive him. He repaid Zeus's kindness by trying to kidnap the god's wife, Hera. Zeus wisely made a copy of Hera out of clouds. Evil Ixion kidnapped the copy by mistake.

Sentence: If caught he will be tied to a wheel of fire which will roll across heaven for all time.

Reward: Free cloud-model of Hera, autographed by its maker, Zeus.

WANTED

3 Name: Phaethon

Wanted for: Driving without due care and attention. This young man begged Helios to let him drive the Sun across the sky in Helios's chariot. When Helios handed over the controls the young joy-rider Phaethon began showing off. He drove so low that the sun scorched the Earth.

Sentence: If caught he will be struck dead by a thunderbolt from Zeus and then be banned from driving for three years.

Reward: Free trip to the sun.

WANTED

4 Name: Midas

Wanted for: Manslaughter (accidental killing). This greedy king was not satisfied with the wealth of his kingdom. He asked the gods for the gift of turning whatever he touched into gold. When he touched his daughter she turned into a solid gold statue. She is gilt and her father is guilty.

Sentence: If caught he will be sentenced to have his ears turned into ass's ears so the world will know how foolish he is.

Reward: One solid gold statue of a princess.

WANTED

5 Name: Narcissus

Wanted for: Breach of promise. This extremely handsome young man made several young women to fall in love with him. Then he rejected them because he was more in love with himself. As a result young women like Echo faded away and died.

Sentence: If caught he will be made to sit by a calm pool, fall in love with his own reflection and die of a broken heart too. He will travel to the Underworld and stay in love with his reflection in the River Styx.

Reward: Free mirror

WANTED

◊ **Name:** Tantalus

Wanted for: Theft and cannibalism. Stole the food of the gods. Then he invited them to a feast. To test if they really knew everything he killed his son and served him in a stew to the gods.

Sentence: If caught he will stand in a pool of water with fruit hanging just out of reach. If he tries to eat or drink, the fruit or water will move out of his way so he will be hungry and thirsty for ever.

Reward: A free carton of Ambrosia, food of the gods

WANTED

7 **Name:** King Lycaon

Wanted for: Insulting the gods. Lycaon had been a dreadful ruler and ignored all the gods' orders to make his people worship the gods. He even served human flesh to Zeus when he visited Lycaon's kingdom.

Sentence: If caught he will be turned into a wolf, his family will be exterminated (even though they are innocent) and the human race will be almost exterminated by a great flood that will cover the whole Earth.

Reward: A place on the Ark.

WANTED

8 Name: Sceiron

Wanted for: Illegal wrestling. Sceiron stops travellers on the road to Athens. He sits on the narrow ledge of the cliff road and asks the traveller to wash his feet. When the kindly traveller bends down then Sceiron boots them over the edge of the cliff into the sea.

Sentence: If caught he will be thrown over his own cliff into the sea and changed into a rock so the waves will wash over him forever.

Reward: A bucket and spade and a trip to the seaside to watch the execution.

WANTED

9 Name: Procne

Wanted for: Arson. Procne lost her temper with her husband, the vicious Tereus. She cut the throat of their son, cooked him and fed him to Tereus. When Tereus asked about the delicious meat she threw the head of their son at his feet. She also set fire to their house and ran off before Tereus could catch her and punish her.

Sentence: If caught she will be turned into a swallow. Procne will then be chased for all time by a hoopoe – a bird with a long orange bill – knowing it is really her husband with a rusty sword.

Reward: A free fire extinguisher.

WANTED

10 Name: Polycrates

Wanted for: Fraud. Polycrates was king when his kingdom was threatened by the Spartan armies. He agreed to pay them to go away. In fact he gave them lead bars painted to look like gold.

Sentence: If caught he will be handed over to his enemies who will almost certainly crucify him.

Reward: A box of gold (or maybe gold-painted lead bars).

In fact all of these criminals were caught, you will be pleased to hear. The sentences described were the ones carried out.

Legend 2: The Odyssey

Of the top 10 Greek legends the top 2 are connected to the same event – the Trojan War. Most historians agree there really was a Trojan War in which an army from Greece destroyed the city of Troy after a long siege.

But this was in the days before written history. The story was passed down by word of mouth and the truth about Troy became mixed up with the old legends. Real soldiers became super-heroes. The whole story was about humans struggling to survive against the power of the gods.

The story was written down about three hundred years after it happened in 1200 BC. It was written in the form of two poems called the *Iliad* and the *Odyssey*. The writer was someone known as Homer – though "Homer" could have been a team of two or more poets.

Most people like a good horror story – like *Dracula* or *Frankenstein*, where people battle against monsters. Many readers like an adventurous travel story like *Treasure Island* where characters meet dangers in unusual places before returning safely home. Some of the most popular stories, like *Wizard of Oz*, are about the struggles a character has just to get back home.

So it's no wonder the *Odyssey* has been one of the world's most popular stories for almost three thousand years. It's a horror-adventure-travel story about a mighty struggle to get home!

For once the gods are not the important characters – though they are always there, watching over the action and sometimes interfering a little. The important characters are the Greek men and women. And the main character in the *Odyssey* is the hero Odysseus.

Odysseus set off to fight in the Trojan War and was told by an oracle that he would be away from home for twenty years. The war took just ten years but the journey home took another ten years. This was partly because the sea god, Poseidon, had it in for Odysseus and sent storms that drove the Greek ship all over the place from one danger to another.

The story of the Trojan war is told in the *Iliad*. The story of Odysseus's ten-year journey home is told in Homer's second poem, the *Odyssey*. The poem describes the problems back in the home of Odysseus since he has been away so long. It ends with Odysseus returning home to sort out those problems by killing the men who have been causing all the trouble. But the middle part of the poem is about the travels of Odysseus. One of the most famous adventures is about his meeting with a monster from your nightmares – the Cyclops.

This was a one-eyed giant who would shake you warmly by the throat and say, "Hello . . . I'm pleased to eat you!"

The monster muncher*

The Cyclops, Polyphemus, was a shepherd on an isle,
He watched his sheep in sunshine and in rain.
Like all his Cyclops brothers he had just one centre eye,
And like the rest, he'd very little brain.

The Cyclops were all giants, each was taller than a house,
They never washed their feet and smelled quite vile.
They lived in caves and cooked themselves great pots of
mutton stew,
But the thought of eating humans made them smile.

So just imagine when old Polyphemus came back home
And found a dozen humans! He was jolly.
"We are the great Greek heroes on our way from Troy,"
they said.
"Hello," he growled, "You chaps can call me Polly!"

The giant stretched a hand out, and he grabbed a
human leg,
He lifted one man up and swung him round.
The man began to scream in fear, but not for very long,
For the giant dashed his head against the ground.

*Read this aloud for extra enjoyment.

152

Then Polyphemus raised the man and popped him in his
mouth,
He smacked his lips, the cave rang with his laughter.
Next he grabbed a second man and held him in his fist.
"Your friend was nice – so I'll have you for afters!"

Next morning giant Polly woke. He stretched and said,
"Hello!
I think I'll have my breakfast here in bed!"
He swept a mighty hand around the cave and grabbed a
man.
He raised him up . . . and dropped him on his head.

After breakfast Polyphemus rolled away the stone,
And led his sheep out for a grassy munch.
He put the boulder firmly back and trapped the men inside,
He'd come and eat another two for lunch.

The men turned to their leader, great Odysseus was his
name,
And begged him, "Boss! Please come up with a plan!
If we don't get away from here we'll all be dead and gone.
He'll eat us, every single living man."

Odysseus was a clever chap, and great at making plans.
He'd saved his men already on this trip.
They took a mighty tree trunk that was lying in the cave
And carved it to a sharply pointed tip.

They'd stored up two great barrels of their very strongest
wine -
(Brought down from their own ship the day before.)
The men were lying ready and they all knew what to do,
As the giant Polly rolled away the door.

The Cyclops ate two more men, then Odysseus said, "Dear
sir,
We'd like to offer you some wine to drink."
The Cyclops swallowed up a barrel in a single gulp.
And smacked his lips, "That's tasty stuff, I think!"

The Greeks passed another barrel to big Polyphemus,
And in no time at all that wine was gone.
At last he fell back drunk and giggled, "Hey, what is your
name?"
Odysseus said, "Dear sir, my name's No One!"

The giant mumbled, "Let me tell you, No One is my friend.
I like No One . . . No One is my pet.
When I eat these humans I'll leave No One until last."
Odysseus said, "You'll eat no one, I bet!"

As Poly slept the Greeks picked up their tree trunk like a
spear,
They heated it until the tip glowed white.
They raised it up and thrust it down into the giant's eye.
He woke to find he was as blind as night.

Then Polyphemus screamed with pain, and clutched at his
lost eye,
His Cyclops brothers on the isle came running.
They stood outside his boulder door and called to their big mate;
And that's where sly Odysseus' plan was cunning.

One Cyclops cried "Who's hurt you?" and of course the
giant fool
Said "No One's done it . . . No One's hurt my eye!"
No One should be punished and there's No One here to blame!
His brothers shrugged and left him there to cry.

So next morning Polyphemus rolled the boulder back again
To let his sheep walk out and feed on grass.
But he groped around the doorway with his blind and mighty
hands,
To make quite sure no Greeks could ever pass.

But still the sly Odysseus had a plan to get away,
Beneath each sheep he tied one of his men.
The blinded Cyclops missed them as each clung onto a fleece.
Until the Greeks found freedom once again.

And so Odysseus and his crew survived another danger.
They took their bearings, setting course for home.
But what Odysseus didn't know was just what lay ahead.
He still had many years and miles to roam.

Now if you wander through those seas and come to Cyclops'
Isle,
 . Don't panic if they catch you . . . and don't cry.
Just take a pole and heat it till the end is glowing hot,
And poke the evil giant in the eye!

Of course, Odysseus finally arrived home, reclaimed his land and saved his wife from the vicious men who were trying to marry her and take his wealth.

Maybe that's why the *Odyssey* is the number 2 Greek legend! It's one of the few to actually have a happy ending!

Top Facts 2: Legendary words

Greek legends have been around for thousands of years and they are still with us today . . . in some ways you might not imagine. For example, some of the stories and the characters have given us words that we still use today. For example, many people describe a long journey as an *odyssey* after Homer's poem.

Here are ten words that come from Greek legends, but only one of the three explanations is actually true.

You can turn this into a game for two teams of three.

Each team takes one word in turn. They then give the opposition three possible meanings for the word – only one of which is true. The opposition try to guess which of the three is correct. Then it's the turn of the other team to guess.

If you don't want to play it as a game then simply test yourself. How many can you score out of the following ten?

Top ten teaser

1   *Panic* (meaning a sudden fear turning you out of control)
A)   From the story of Perseus who used a polished frying pan to look at the head of the Gorgon. If you look at the horror in the reflection of the pan then you will have a sudden fear – a pan-fear or a panic.
B)   From the god of spiders, Panicus. He would lower himself down beside victims like Little Miss Muffet and cause them to cry,

"*panicus!*" . . . and panic.

C) From the god Pan. Greek shepherds often saw their flocks rush around in fear for no reason at all. The shepherds blamed the god Pan for causing the disturbance.

2 **Volcano** (a mountain that explodes with hot ash and lava)

A) From the god of fire, Hephaestus. His home and his blacksmith's workshop is inside a volcano. The Greeks called him Hephaestus but the Romans changed his name to Vulcan.

B) From the god of anger, Volcan. When a volcano erupts it is said to be the god Volcan losing his temper.

C) From the Greek word meaning "cooker". The gods fried their giant eggs for breakfast in giant frying pans held over a giant cooker – a volcano.

3 **Cereal** (a grain that grows and can be harvested for food)

A) From the Greek goddess Cerea who makes the

gods their breakfasts (cooked with Perseus's pan over a volcano). Breakfast foods, cereals, were named after Cerea.

B) The goddess of corn, Demeter, is taken to the Underworld for one third of the year – then we have winter. When she is on Earth her warmth lets crops crow. The crops are "cereals" because the Roman name for Demeter is "Ceres".

C) From the Greek word "*cerea*" meaning "a play about the gods". Audiences would see one part of the play each day of the week. It was a "cereal".

4 *Hypnotize* (send someone to sleep)

A) A Greek poet called Hypnos was so boring that when he started reciting legends all of his audience fell asleep.

B) The Greek god of sleep was Hypnos – he is the son of "night" and when night arrives sleep is not far behind.

C) The Greek word Hypnos meant hip. If a rich Greek could not get to sleep he would send for a "hip-no-twist" – this man would be paid to stand and swing his leg backwards and forwards like a pendulum. This would soon send the rich Greek to sleep.

5   ***Lethal*** (meaning "deadly")

A)   From the Greek god of the Underworld, Leather, a tough-skinned character who would take you from this Earth and drag you to his kingdom of the Underworld.

B)   From a Greek word meaning "sword". A parent would often warn a child, "That sword is deadly" or, in Greek, "That lethal is lethal".

C)   From the river of the Underworld "Lethe". The word means "sleepy" and if you sleep really deeply then you are in the Underworld river of Lethe – you are dead.

6   ***Syringe*** (a medical instrument for giving injections)

A)   From the Greek nymph Syrinx. When the girl was chased by the god Pan she disguised herself as a hollow reed. This hollow reed is similar to the hollow needle that doctors invented to give injections. They named their hollow needle after the hollow-reed girl, Syrinx.

B)   Doctors invented hollow needles to suck blood samples from patients. They named the hollow sucking needle after the Greek god Syrinx. Syrinx was easily fooled – like the needle he was a "sucker" in fact, so the needle is named after him.

C)   From the Greek word meaning "sharp, painful
        torture". Doctors enjoy giving the sharp painful
        torture of injections so they used the Greek
        word.

7   **Siren** (an instrument for making a loud wailing
        noise)

A)   From the Siren women who used their sad and
        wailing songs to attract sailors. Of course, when
        the sailors came nearer they ran aground on the
        rocks around the Sirens' island and the Sirens
        ate them.

B)   From the god Sirenus. Zeus became annoyed
        with Sirenus and turned him into the north
        wind. When the north wind moans down your
        chimney you can her the voice of Sirenus – a
        siren.

C)   From the Greek word meaning "danger". The
        Greeks saw a raid coming and cried "Siren!
        Siren!" or "Danger! Danger!" Modern countries
        used a machine to warn of air raids – when the
        air-raid siren wails it means "Danger! Danger!"

8   ***Demon*** (an evil spirit)

A)   From the god of evil Damon. At first he was the only evil god. Soon he had lots of children and he named them all after himself. Then there were lots of little Damons – or Demons.

B)   From the god of the Olympics, Damon. He was the god of speed and people used to say, "Gosh! He's a fast little Damon" as their child scuttered across the floor. Soon this came to mean "little devil". (Racing driver Graham Hill named his son Damon because he wanted him to grow up blessed by Damon, god of Speed.)

C)   From the Greek word for a little Greek god or a spirit messenger from the greater gods. Everyone in Ancient Greece had two "demons" – one who carried good messages to you and one who carried bad. When Christians came along they believed all spirits were evil so demon came to mean "evil spirit".

9   ***Money***

A)   From the god of the Moon, Mooney. The Moon was round and silver and so were the Greek coins. "I'll pay you a Mooney" meant "I'll pay you money".

B)   From the Greek word "moaner". Beggars on the streets of Athens used to cry out; "Moan! Moan!

Moan!" People used to pay "moaney" coins to shut them up.

C) From the Greek goddess Hera. The Romans called her Moneta and they began making silver coins in the temple of Moneta. Moneta coins became "money".

10 *Atlas* (map book)

A) From the Greek word meaning "plan". An Atlas book was a "plan" book of the Greek world.

B) From the god Atlantis. This god sailed across the sea named after him – the Atlantic. He returned and said he'd discovered America but not even Zeus believed him. He drew a book of maps to show his journey – an Atlantis book – and everyone said he'd just made it up. The tormented god went back to America and the Statue of Liberty is a life-sized model of him.

C) From the god Atlas. In early Greek legends he carried the sky on his back. A book of maps published in 1595 was called an Atlas after the god. The map-maker, a man called Mercator, made a silly mistake. He thought that Atlas carried the Earth on his back and his book of maps showed what Atlas the god was carrying.

Answers

1-C, 2-A, 3-B, 4-B, 5-C, 6-A, 7-A, 8-C, 9-C, 10-C

Legend 1: The Trojan War

Thanks to Homer's poems we know a lot about the Trojan legends. Three thousand years later the poems are still being printed and still being read. The *Iliad* and the *Odyssey* aren't just top of the top 10 Greek legends – they are the top stories of *all time*! Everyone has heard about the siege of Troy and the famous wooden horse trick. The Trojan War is the number 1 story in our top 10.

This was a war where the gods took sides and helped their favourites. Men did most of the killing while women made most of the trouble.

It all started when Prince Paris of Troy was asked to judge a beauty competition between the goddesses Hera, Athena and Aphrodite. Aphrodite won and gave Paris a special present – the love of the most beautiful woman on Earth. That's when the trouble started. Because the most beautiful woman on Earth was Helen – and she was already married to King Menelaus of Sparta. And it was trouble because the losers in the beauty competition, Hera and Athena, were out to get their revenge on Prince Paris and revenge on Troy.

Prince Paris paid a visit to King Menelaus, met Helen and kidnapped her. The furious king gathered an army of Greek heroes and set off to Troy to get her back.

They fought for nine years with lots of death and misery, but no result. That's when the story of the first poem, the *Iliad*, starts. There are several stories about the war . . . not just the wooden horse. Here's one about the Greek hero Achilles.

Later the Greeks invented the theatre and turned many of the Trojan War stories into plays. If the *Iliad* had been written by a playwright of the time then the Achilles scenes might have gone something like this . . .

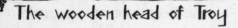

The wooden head of Troy

Cast:

Chorus: A narrator who knows everything.

Achilles: Super hero with just one teeny weakness

Patroclus: Achilles' best mate

Thetis: Sea nymph and mother of Achilles

Agamemnon: Brother of Menelaus and commander of the Greeks

Helen: Wife of Menelaus, stolen by Paris, most beautiful woman in the world

Paris: Prince of Troy, kidnapper of Helen

Hector: Trojan Champ

<u>Scene 1:</u> In the Greek camp

Chorus: Here we are in the Greek camp. These are not happy campers, believe me. You see the

169

Greek leader, Agamemnon, had captured a Trojan girl called Chryseis and refused to give her back. The gods sent a plague to sicken the Greek army. The Greeks' best fighter, Achilles, tried to persuade Agamemnon to give her back. Because they were great heroes they discussed this as great heroes should . . .

Achilles: Give the girl back you daft old bat.

Agamemnon: Shan't, shan't, shan't! I saw her first. I get to keep her.

Achilles: Give her back to the Trojans or I'll smack you in the mouth.

Agamemnon: That's your answer to everything. Violence. You're just a big bully.

Achilles: I'm not!

Agamemnon: You are!

Achilles: Not!

Agamemnon: Are!

Achilles: Our men are dying of the plague!

Agamemnon: Our men are dying of boredom.

We've been here nine years and you can't even beat the pathetic Paris.

Achilles: Me! Me? I'm not the leader. *You* are!

Agamemnon: Ah, but you're supposed to be the *hero*. Why don't you go and do some heroics, eh?

Achilles: I need my men behind me and they're dying of the plague. Give that Chryseis girl back or I'll stick my sword right up your nose.

Agamemnon: Right! That's it! I'll give her back to the Trojans. But I'll also give back your slave girl Briseis at the same time.

Achilles: *My* slave girl! Keep her out of it.

Agamemnon: Shan't. If I'm losing Chryseis then you're losing Briseis. That's only fair.

Achilles: It's not.

Agamemnon: 'Tis. Anyway, I'm the leader so you have to do what you're told.

171

Chryseis goes back and so does Briseis.

Achilles: Fine by me. Just when it comes to the next fight don't ask me for help. I'm packing up my tent and going somewhere else.

Agamemnon: You can't do that!

Achilles: Just watch me, mate.

Chorus: So the leader and the hero fell out over two Trojan women. Without Achilles the Greek army started to do really badly. Finally they were driven back to their ships . . .

Scene 2:   **On the beach**

Agamemnon: Patroclus! Patroclus! What are we going to do? You're Achilles' best mate. Can you not persuade him to come back and fight?

Patroclus: I tried, boss. He refused.

Agamemnon: Did you offer him my gifts?

Patroclus: He said if you offered him as many gifts as there are grains of sand he still wouldn't come back.

Agamemnon: Then we're up the creek without a paddle, Patroclus.

Patroclus: Not quite, boss. I have an idea!

Agamemnon: An idea?

Patroclus: An idea. Achilles *did* say I could borrow his armour. When the Trojans see me in Achilles' armour they'll think *I'm* Achilles. They'll all run away!

Agamemnon: Good thinking, Patroclus. It just might work!

Chorus: Of course it didn't work. Patroclus put on the armour, he stepped onto the battlefield and came helmet to helmet with the hero of Troy, Hector.

Hector: Oh, look! It's Achilles! I've waited nine years to get my hands on him. Come here, Achilles!

Patroclus: What?

Hector: I said come here, Achilles.

Patroclus: Who?

Hector: Achilles! You *are* Achilles, aren't you?

Patroclus: Oh . . . er . . . yes! I'm Achilles and you're supposed to run away.

Hector: Why?

Patroclus: 'Cos you're scared of me.

Hector: No I'm not.

Patroclus: You're not?

Hector: I'm not. In fact, I'm going to kill you.

Patroclus: Er . . . in that case, I'm not Achilles. I'm a fake, a phoney, a stooge and a stand-in.

Hector: And you're a dead man.

Patroclus: I thought you might say that. Have you no mercy?

Hector:	*(As he stabs him)* No.
Patroclus:	Ouch! Have you no pity?
Hector:	*(As he stabs again)* No.
Patroclus:	Ouch! Have you no glasses? Can't you see I'm Patroclus?
Hector:	Ooops! Sorry, old chap. Easy mistake to make. Have a nice funeral.
Patroclus:	Thanks. *(Staggers off to die)*

<u>Scene 3:</u>   **Achilles' tent**

Chorus: When Achilles heard his best friend was dead he was upset.

Achilles: Boo-hoo! Boo-hoo! Booey-hooey!

Chorus: His mother, the sea nymph Thetis, came to cheer him up.

Thetis: Never mind, my pet. I've had the blacksmith god Hephaestus make you some new armour. Go and kill a few hundred Trojans. It'll make you feel better.

Achilles: What if they kill me first, mum?

Thetis: Why, bless me! They can't kill you my little cherub! Didn't you know. When you were born I dipped you in the River Styx. I held you by your little heel and dunked you in.

177

Achilles:	And that means I can't be hurt by human weapons?
Thetis:	Not unless someone hits you in the heel, and that's not very likely, is it?
Achilles:	No mum.
Thetis:	So, off you go, kill that nasty Hector and you'll feel a lot better.
Achilles:	Thanks mum.
Thetis:	That's my little treasure-chops.
Chorus:	So Achilles went off and met Hector under the walls of Troy.

Scene 4: **Under the walls of Troy.**

Achilles: You Hector?

Hector: Who's asking?

Achilles: I'm asking.

Hector: Who's "I'm"?

Achilles: I'm *Achilles* . . . and you killed my *friend* and I'm very *angry*.

Hector: Sorry, mate. I thought it was you.

Achilles: Well, it's me *now* and I'm going to kill you.

Hector: Do you have to?

Achilles: 'Fraid so.

Hector: In that case you'll have to catch me first! *(Runs off)*

Chorus: Achilles chased Hector three times round the walls of Troy before Hector stopped running and faced Achilles. Achilles stabbed him in the throat with a spear, tied him to his chariot and dragged the body round the outside of the walls. The Greeks were thrilled. But the Trojans were very upset. From their view point on top of the thick walls of the city, Paris and Helen were worried . . .

<u>Scene 5:</u> **The walls of Troy**

Helen: I'm worried, Paris, worried. Hector's dead and that nasty Achilles has made a right mess of his body.

Paris: It's nothing to what they'll do if they get their hands on *my* body, Helen.

Helen: There are *worse* things than being captured and tortured and mangled and killed you know.

Paris: What's worse than that?

Helen: Imagine what they'd do to *me*!

Paris: What?

Helen: They'd make me go back to Sparta and live as the wife of that awful Menelaus. That's worse than death . . . that's living death!

Paris: True. But what else can we do?

Helen: Well, you could kill that Achilles.

Paris: What? Me? He'd eat me for breakfast. He's a big lad that Achilles and he's very handy with that spear of his.

181

Helen: Look! There he is bending over Hector's body. Get that bow and shoot him in the back.

Paris: In the back? That's cheating a bit, isn't it?

Helen: Would you rather be tortured and mangled?

Paris: You have a good point there. There's just one thing.

Helen: What's that?

Paris: I'm a rotten shot with this bow. I couldn't hit the walls of Troy if I had me nose against it.

Helen: You said it yourself. Achilles is a big lad. Even you couldn't miss a target like that!

Paris: Well, I'll give it a try.

Chorus: So Paris took an arrow, took careful aim . . . and fired.

Helen: Ohhhh! Paris. That was the worst shot I've seen in my life. A blooming great back to aim at and what did you hit?

Paris: Sorry, pet.

Helen: What did you hit?

Paris: His heel, pet.

Helen: His *heel*. He's hardly likely to die of an arrow in the heel, is he?

Paris: Well he's limping around a lot – and it *was* a poisoned arrow.

Helen: He *does* look hurt. And there's an awful lot of blood.

Paris: He's fallen over!

Helen: The doctor's checking his breathing . . . look, they're covering his face! Well, I'll be blowed! He's dead. I always said you were the best shot in the Trojan army.

Paris: Achilles dead! They'll never beat us now! Not if they fight another ninety-nine years!

Helen: Never!

Chorus: Which just goes to show how wrong you can be. The Greeks came up with the famous Wooden Horse trick and finally defeated Troy. Helen was taken back to Sparta and Paris was pulverised. Which just goes to show, you should *always* look a gift horse in the mouth.

THE END

Top Facts 1: Play time

The stories of the Greek gods and Greek heroes were told by poets like Homer. Then something very important happened. One of the poets actually started to pretend to be the main character – he became an "actor".

Other "actors" spoke to the main character as a group (called a "chorus") and then the Greeks had a "play".

Then someone added a second leading character and a third. They raised them up on a platform or "stage" and added scenery behind the actors. The chorus performed their lines in front of the stage. The audience were seated in large rows of stone seats and the Greeks had built the world's first "theatre". Some of these theatres held 20,000 people – more than a lot of British football grounds.

The Greeks enjoyed these plays so much they turned play writing into a competition. Everyone would go along to the competition and watch the plays. The prizes were small but the glory of winning was great.

In time the serious plays about gods and heroes became less popular. The Greeks preferred the comedies with funny stories about ordinary people.

Can you picture the scene in a Greek theatre? Look at these facts and test your teacher or puzzle your parents with the quiz.

The Greek word "*theatron*" meant "watching place" and the Greeks would visit the *theatron* to see the plays. But what would they see when they got there? Simply answer True or False to the following questions . . .

1 The actors wanted to be seen from the back of the *theatron* so they made themselves as large as possible. They walked on stilts and wore padded costumes on their bodies and masks over their faces. True/false?

2 The members of the audience took along candles so the stage would be lit up and they could see the action. True/false?

3 The plays had special effects. Characters like gods or Pegasus the flying horse could float above the stage on ropes. True/false?

4 The actors would stage exciting fights and battles on stage with lots of blood splashed around for effect. True/false?

5 The plays were written as poems.
True/false?

6 Women wore much richer costumes than the men on stage.
True/false?

7 Greek theatre had an "orchestra".
True/false?

8 A Greek playwright would write comedies and tragedies, depending on which competition he wanted to enter.
True/false?

9 The audience got into the Greek theatre performances free of charge.
True/false?

10 The first prize for a winning play was a purse full of gold.
True/false?

187

Answers

1 True The stilts were shoes with large blocks underneath them. The mask could only show one expression, of course, but at least one actor could play several parts by simply changing his mask. Or a character's mask could change in a play like Oedipus – in one scene Oedipus is a powerful king, in the next his eyes have been clawed out with a brooch. The masks would be made from cloth over a wooden frame so they were light and the actor didn't suffocate on warm days. The face on the mask was sometimes made to look like a famous person of the time! Some historians believe the mouth of the mask may have held a small funnel, so the voice of the actor came out louder.

2 False The plays always took place in the daylight. The theatre was an open space and in Greek summers the Sun was warm and bright enough for these outdoor performances.

3 True When the human characters got themselves into a terrible situation the god could be lowered down from a crane to sort out all of their problems. This trick was known as "god from a machine". In comedies the crane could be used for spectacular scene; in a comedy called *Peace* the audience see a giant dung beetle flying over the stage!

4 False The plays had hardly any action in them at all. Characters would not fight on stage . . . instead a character would come on stage and describe what happened: "I've just come from a battle under the walls of Troy. You should have seen it! Achilles took his spear and threw it at Hector . . ." and so on. (See Legend 1, Scene 5.)

5 True The Greeks went to hear great poetry spoken rather than see exciting action on stage. The "Chorus" needed a poem so they could sing it all together – that's much easier if the words have a regular beat of a poem. The Chorus would also dance to the beat.

6 False Women were *never* allowed to act on the stage. They were allowed to watch plays but not take part in them. The women characters were all played by men; the costumes, the long-haired wigs and the faces painted on the masks showed the audience they were playing the part of a woman . . . even if the voice wasn't quite right.

7 True But a Greek orchestra it wasn't a band of musicians as it is today. In Greek times an "orchestra" was a flat circle of grass where the Chorus stood to sing and dance.

8 False The writers of tragedy wrote tragedy, the writers of comedy wrote comedy and they never crossed over. There would be three tragedies chosen each year to be shown in the competition and three comedies. Sometimes there was a competition with five comedies. The competitions would go on for three or four days.

9 True The theatre started as a way of praising of a certain god so it was a religious festival. You wouldn't usually charge someone to go to church and the Greeks never charged anyone to go to the theatre. The costumes and the scripts and the masks and the actors cost money. A rich citizen of the city would usually pay for the whole production.

10 False – probably! No one is quite sure what the prizes for playwrights were, but it is certain that the prizes for the poems in the festival were a bull (first prize), a jar of wine (second) and a goat (third).

Epilogue

Greek legends have been with us for thousands of years and it's a fair bet they'll be with us for a few thousand more. They have everything that good stories should have – excitement, action, surprise, horror and, above all, great characters.

A hundred years from now the people in your television soap operas will be forgotten. But your great-grandchildren will still remember the labours of Heracles, the wanderings of Odysseus, the troubles of Troy and the great, gory, groovy Greek gods on Olympus.

Of course the writers, (like me) will have taken their buckets and spades to paddle by the great River Styx in the Underworld. Human beings come and go. But gods live forever.

I hope you enjoyed the Top 10. If you did then look after them, keep them in your heart and your head and pass them on. Then these stories ought to live forever too.

They deserve to. After all, they are the tops.